Edward Robert Bulwer Lytton

Fables in Song

Edward Robert Bulwer Lytton

Fables in Song

ISBN/EAN: 9783744775670

Printed in Europe, USA, Canada, Australia, Japan

Cover: Foto ©Thomas Meinert / pixelio.de

More available books at **www.hansebooks.com**

FABLES IN SONG

BY

ROBERT LORD LYTTON

AUTHOR OF 'POEMS BY OWEN MEREDITH'

VOL. II.

WILLIAM BLACKWOOD AND SONS
EDINBURGH AND LONDON
MDCCCLXXIV

CONTENTS OF THE SECOND VOLUME.

vi CONTENTS.

ERRATA.

Vol. II., p. 7, 9th line from top of page, *for*
   Should *scarce* such momentary beauty back,
Read
   Should scare such momentary beauty back.

Vol. II., p. 65, *for*
   Fatigue themselves in torturing mankind,
      Get out of breath in running down their prey!
Read
   Get out of breath in running down their prey,
      Fatigue themselves in torturing mankind!

Vol. II., Table of Contents, page vi ; also page 161, title ; and 163, 165, head of pages ; *for* Suum quique *read* Suum cuique.

INTRODUCTORY.

1.

A LITTLE bird fares well in Spring.
  For all she wants she finds enough,
And every casual common thing
  She makes her own without rebuff.

2.

First, wool and hair from sheep and cow :
  Then twig and straw, to bind them fast,
From thicket and from thatch : and now
  A little nest is built at last.

3.

From out that little nest shall rise,
  When woods are warm, a living song,
A music mixt with light, that flies
  Thro' fluttering shade the leaves among.

4.

Its home? straw, twig, and wool, and hair.
Mere nothings, these, to house or herd.
Who made them something, made them fair,
Making them all her own? The bird.

5.

O little bird, take everything,
And build thy nest without rebuff,
And, when thy nest is builded, sing!
For who can praise thy song enough?

6.

And some believe (believe they wrong?)
If like the bird the bard could sing,
That, like the bird, fit home for Song
The bard would find in everything

7.

By casual grace of common chance
From house and herd, from thick and thatch,
Assign'd for Song's inheritance
Had Song the gift that grace to catch.

8.

Such things I found, by passers-by
    As rubbish from the roadside thrust ;
Which poets, seeking poesy,
    Disdain'd to rescue from the dust.

9.

Yet here they are—not rubbish now
    I fain would hope.   Do critics stare,
Reserve applause, and rub the brow ?
    Oh that a little bird I were !

———◆———

XXIX.

FIAT JUSTITIA.

CANTO THE FIRST.—THEORY.

1.

SIMPLICIUS was a man of good condition,
Whose naturally easy disposition
Found in his easy fortunes natural vent.
He, for that reason, was benevolent ;
But tho' he sought to find Benevolence
Efficient sanction in the social sense
Of Justice, much his feelings were offended
By the unsocial, unjust, things that men did.

For, in the world around him, everywhere
He saw but envy, arrogance, and care,
Malice, and fear, oppression, and mistrust,
Anarchic, anti-social, soul-depraving.

2.

" Alas !" he thought, " if men would be but just,
Then life would be for every man worth having !
But, tho', in practice, all of them ignore
What justice claims, in theory, they cry
' *Fiat justitia !*' adding evermore
' *Pereat mundus !*'   *Pereat mundus*, why ?
Wherefore a *pereat* to this glorious world,
Which cordially to all of us cries *vivat ?*
Far be from me that hateful *pereat* hurl'd !
The goal 'tis my ambition to arrive at
Is Justice and Enjoyment too, combined."

3.

Oft hath the love of justice caused confusion,
And much this thought disturb'd the good man's mind,
Until it brought him to the strange conclusion
That Nature in befitting form presents
To every man himself turn'd inside out ;
So that we contemplate our own contents
In beast and bird.   Now this belief, no doubt,
Was the blind offspring of imagination,
But, as for him, it help'd him to become

Quite comfortable with the whole creation ;
For, when he walk'd abroad, he felt at home.

4.

Thus, if in sight a shy deer chanced to flit
Down some dim glade, scarce seen ere gone again.
"'Tis it!" he murmur'd, "I remember it ;
A timid thought, that long about my brain
I've noticed lurking. Pity, the world's pack
With boisterous bark, whene'er it steals in view,
Should scare such momentary beauty back ;
So fair its flittings, and, alas, so few !"
Or he would muse, when, home at eve to stall,
He watch'd the slow kine wend their wonted way,
" Lo, life's tame habitudes ! whose footsteps fall
Along the self-same pastures every day,
And, every night, by the same trodden traces
Of usage, back to the same commonplaces.
Dull plodders these ! Their placid life goes pat
Only whilst round them, comfortably creast,
Clings Custom's garb, wherein they all grow fat.
Freedom is death to each domestic beast.
The wolf and fox are better off in that.
They for themselves know how to shift at least.
Adventurous liberty is theirs. That's much.
For, tho' they use it but to rob and kill,
The world would languish wanting some such touch
Of vagabond and savage instinct. Still
The wild beast passion for adventure wild

We all have in us, hide it how we will.
And when I see a white dove, plump and mild,
I understand the vulture.   Nature mocks
Man's passions with pathetic paradox ;
Sweet simple Innocence can never quite
Our torpid sympathies from slumber stir,   .
Nor hold our interest in her at the height,
Till things are going not quite well with her."

5.

From these examples, which are not capricious,
Of how his witless fancy wander'd on,
Sagacious readers may perceive Simplicius
Was, certes, somewhat of a simpleton.
Tho' not, for that, worse off than his judicious
And candid friends who labour'd to disclose
The fallacies he cherish'd unsuspicious ;
And lost their labour, as you may suppose.
For aye, the poorer that he is, the more
A man fights hard to keep, in purse or pate,
Prolong'd possession of his little store.
Whereon the world remarks, in tones irate,
(As tho' itself were perfect on the score
Of yielding to beliefs that will not mate
With those which it was wont to hold before)
" Stupidity is always obstinate !"
But surely they, whose stock of wits is small,
Do well to grasp it with resolved rigidity ;
For, if a man be stupid, no endeavour

Upon your part to break down the stolidity
His instinct builds about him like a wall
Can, even if successful, make him clever;
And, if you take from him his own stupidity,
You leave him nothing of his own at all.

6.

This man had much that, without contradiction,
He call'd his own : and, notably his plan
For making justice upon earth no fiction.
" For wherefore with his fellow-men is man,"
Simplicius ask'd, " accustom'd to resort?
'Tis for their qualities, we must surmise.
I mean, their good ones : since where these fall short
Man shuns his fellows.   But all men comprise
Within them qualities that ill comport
One with the other, and in turn each tries
To spoil the rest.   The beasts have naught to do
But to embody each some part of man ;
Which, for that reason, in each beast we view
More pleasurably perfect than it can
By any possibility be found
In man himself ; whose qualities, ill-pack't,
Jumble each other in their narrow bound,
And muddle his humanity in fact.
For instance.   I've a mineral collection
Of costly crystals, perfect in all parts ;
And, in it, specimens, that fill one section,
Of felspar, and of mica, and of quartz.

This granite block (the bench whereon I sit)
Hath, as by close inspection I divine,
The self-same minerals mixt up in it.
But what a difference between these and mine !
The sparkling columns of my quartz o'erthrown,
And pounded into powder ! every bit
Of my poor felspar, featureless ! each crown
Of my fine mica's fairy foliation
Crumpled into amalgamated grit !
The whole—a dull disturb'd crystallisation,
Where nothing is as it would fain have been !
So man.   Not so the simpler beasts, I ween.
What's Charm? The bird. And what is Grace! The cat.
What is Fidelity ?   The dog.   I know
(And I confess that I am grieved thereat)
These creatures eat each other.   But even so
Conflicting virtues live in man ; no less
Discordantly than cat and dog together ;
Striving each other's merits to suppress.
Grace, if she catch it, leaves not Charm a feather,
Whilst she herself, unless she can contrive
To scratch his eyes out, by Fidelity
Is maul'd to death, or merely left alive
A wreck of bones.   Can Prejudice say why ?"

7.

For all these reasons, since Simplicius thought
The best companions that a man can have
Are innocence and charm together brought,

Fidelity, and grace, and humour grave,
A bird, and cat, and dog, and bear, he bought :
But kept them each apart, exclaiming—" *Fiat*
Justitia, vivat mundus,—beast and man, too !"
The special qualities he set so high at
The culminating point of each *pro tanto,*
As well as some defects he wink'd his eye at,
Are faithfully set forth in our next Canto.

CANTO THE SECOND.—PRACTICE.

1.

Charm, in a blackbird's brazen cage confined,
Was somewhat shy and wild at first of all.
But to his lot the bird became resign'd,
When daily to that favour'd lot did fall
Fine sand, fresh water, and luxurious bits
Of bullock's heart, that deck'd the cage's slits,
As venison, scenting gusts that keep it pure,
Hangs in the larder of an epicure ;
With carrots, cut in slices, eggs of ants,
Maggots, and all things that a blackbird wants,
For dainty relish of his daily fare.

2.

Here be it said that to his first essay
Simplicius, though no doubt a doctrinaire,

Applied his doctrine in a general way,
And prudently decided to forbear
From pushing to extremes its leading principle.
For, since reformers fail when they attempt
At making Justice all at once invincible,
He from her jurisdiction left exempt
(As minor matters which he took no heed of)
The grubs, and eggs, and worms, his bird had need of.
The grateful Bird lived, happier day by day,
A life harmonious with its lot quotidian ;
And, if 'twas still an elegy, his lay
Had notes, at least, more joyous than Ovidian.

3.

As for the fluffy, puffy, plump white Cat,
If *she* were not completely comfortable,
There surely never was a diplomat
Half such a humbug, half so slyly able
To simulate the feelings he should feel,
And those he feels, and should not, to conceal.
The chief part of her life-long holiday
(As tho' it were her only care on earth
To keep her soft self warm) a clump she lay
Of cream-white languid limbs beside the hearth ;
Or rubb'd her lithe back in a flattering bow
Against the legs of her good lord and master,
Smoothing those spotless flakes of furry snow
In which, for whiteness, not Mont Blanc surpass'd
    her ;

Or, in the firelight's fluctuating glow,
Curl'd on his lap and safe from all disaster,
She purr'd as tho' she to herself, half-sleeping,
Were telling o'er her dreams in drowsy tone ;
Or else, about the chairs and tables leaping,
(A frolic phantom scarcely seen ere gone)
She whisk'd, and frisk'd, and flitted here and there,
Fitful as fancy, and as childhood fair.

4.

To these two qualities of Charm and Grace
Which he in Bird and Cat together got,
Simplicius added, in the third good place,
Fidelity—so true, man finds it not
Save in a dog. The Dog of our Simplicius
Was great and good ; and well deserved, poor fellow,
A name less ominous of deeds flagitious
Than chance had given him—say Philax, Bello,
Or Lion, even, or Turk—for he was bold
(Albeit without a touch of temper vicious)
But Nero ? . . . cramm'd with cruelties untold,
Whose character was, like his name, nigritious,
—A name recalling murders manifold !
Such was the name this dog, by chance capricious,
Had been baptised with, when, but three months old,
His tender age might, sure, have guaranteed him
Against the libellous title thus decreed him.

5.

If pure gold, oozed from out the Age of Gold,
Could, in a living form, have glow'd on earth,
None better fitted to present, and hold
Unsullied, its primæval perfect worth
Could earth have found it, than our Nero's own ;
Nor more in colour kindred to the hue
Whereby that noble metal may be known.
For tawny-colour'd was our Nero too,
As gold is : short-hair'd, all a yellow brown ;
Save for a single streak of glossy black
That, with straightforward purpose, went right down
The whole length of his honourable back,
And his most eloquently honest tail ;
Which wagg'd warm welcome to the world all round.
Black, too, and bright as brightly burnisht mail,
The single star that his fair forehead crown'd,
And black his muzzle was : the unshell'd snail
No blacker shines, whose damp and jetty sheen
Jewels the fresh stalks of the rain-drench'd fennel.
When Nero, his stoop'd head flat-based between
Firm-planted forepaws, peeping from his kennel,
Lay stretch'd sedate in soothing noontide sleep;
Whilst loyal vigilance unlull'd and keen
(No sound escaping its quick silent comment)
Still linger'd in the watchful tremulous wink
Of drowsy lids that twitch'd at every moment,
And duty sat in serious wrinkles deep
Across his brow's sagacious breadth,—I think

That had some Attic sculptor seen that sight,
Grasping his chisel with an eager hand,
He would have cried, in satisfied delight,
" Behold the perfect sculpturesque expression
Of PROPERTY!" And, forced to understand
The imprudence of his wonted prepossession
Against the law of Moses and the land,
A thief, perchance, some honest awe might feel,
And pass on murmuring "Thou shalt not steal!"

6.

Between Fidelity, and Charm, and Grace,
For Humour of a grave and thoughtful kind,
In ursine form, long while a vacant place
Simplicius kept before he chanced to find
Its fit incumbent.   For the ursine race,
Whose sage demeanour and prodigious force
Might with the race of man have long competed
Had they but chosen to dispute man's course,
Have, far from man, to hermit haunts retreated,
And lone they dwell among the mountains lonely.
Man boasts, as tho' the trick must needs endear him
To all four-footed animals at least,
That he can go upon his hind paws only.
For this, and for his faculty to feast
Upon all kinds of food, the beasts revere him
As being the most universal beast.
But in these two respects the Bear comes near him ;
Tho' differing in a third (and not, I fear

To man's advantage) namely in good-nature.
O Timon! Timon! hadst thou been a bear,
Those maledictions, by a human creature
On human creatures hurl'd, not even despair
Would then have wrung from thy resentment.   Guile,
Deceit, and treachery, and treason black
Bruin (for so was named in simple style
This shaggy much-tried sage) had known, alack,
In all their hateful human forms, long while
Ere from a filthy vagrant Bosniac
Simplicius bought him—unembitter'd yet,
And so good-natured that across his back
He let a pert and pranksome monkey get,
Pretend to ride him, and, impetuous, smack
A saucy whip.   Himself a minuet
With sad and stately gesture sometimes deign'd
To dance to music rude of drum and fife,
Tho' oft the mirth of vulgar crowds profaned
This melancholy pastime of a life
Which had known better days.   Alas poor Bruin!
A trustful nature and, for safe fruition,
A love, too fond—of honey—proved his ruin.
Rogues had imposed on his sweet disposition
And made him smart for it.   But Fortune now
Seem'd on his fate to smile with fairer brow.
Simplicius built him in the castle court
A spacious mansion for his calm resort.
Rail'd parapets of stone did there environ
His sleeping chamber girt with grates of iron.
And, in the midst of this deep-sunk domain,

A dead tree, planted by man's labour fast,
Served for his perch whene'er the sage was fain
(Like " Science in her speculative tower ")
A general glance around the world to cast,
With soul unbounded by his lonely bower.

7.

So in Simplicius' hospitable hall
Did Grace and Charm, its daily inmates, dwell.
And, round about those happy precincts, all
Went blithe and " merry as a marriage bell."
The Bird " his native wood-notes warbled wild."
The Cat, like some white curl'd-up humming shell,
Purr'd by the hearth contentment calm and mild.
The Dog bark'd welcome loud and wagg'd delight
To his approving master morn and night.
And he, the blissful owner of these joys,
When he, at any moment, felt inclined
To meditative moods, whose charm decoys
From shallower pleasures oft the pensive mind,
Would sit and muse above that bear-pit wide.
Whence many a mournful monitory growl
With solemn music stirr'd and edified
To heights sublime his contemplative soul.
Sullen it was, nay surly seem'd the sound.
But surly too, nor feebly feminine,
Is that majestic charm by fancy found
In Melancholy's deep and sullen eyne
What time she doth a manly sex assume.

And that is why, when either love or wine
In manly bosoms breeds ungenial gloom,
Chilling with churlish scowl some revel garish,
We call such melancholy conduct—bearish.

CANTO THE THIRD.—EXPERIENCE.

1.

This pleasant life, so calm and so caressing,
Was interrupted by a journey brief
Simplicius, on account of business pressing,
Was forced to undertake. Before the chief
His castle left, he call'd into his presence
An old retainer born beneath its roof,
Of all domestic virtues the quintessence ;
A tried and trusted spirit—above proof.
Whom (to secure administrative unity)
With counsel carefully minute and clear
He gave in charge of his beloved community,
The Dog, the Cat, the Blackbird, and the Bear.

2.

The business settled to his satisfaction
Which drew Simplicius from his own abode,
He, with a mind relieved from all distraction
And full of longings, on his homeward road

One evening reach'd, when it was somewhat late,
The last post station. 'Twas a tiny town,
But few hours distant from his own estate.
But there, his horses having broken down,
For fresh relays he was constrain'd to wait.
Besides, a storm was coming on. So, there
Resolving prudently to pass the night,
He order'd rooms and supper at THE BEAR ;
A little hostel cheerful, clean, and bright,
Whose landlord was postmaster of the village,
A farmer, too, with land in his own tillage.

3.

The candles lighted, and the clean cloth spread,
The curtains drawn in cosier proximity
About the smooth sheets of the snowy bed,
For pure dreams shelter'd by demurest dimity ;
Dandling his napkin with important air
The obsequious waiter offer'd to Simplicius,
Proud of its length, a boastful bill of fare,
And list of wines, which he declared delicious.
Careless as tho' it were a begging letter
Simplicius glanced it over ; and, because
He trusted not its pledge of viands better,
He was about to order without pause
A simple steak—when these words proved a whetter
To his attention—' *Bear's paws, Tartar sauce.*'

4.

This dish to him was quite a novel one.
There is no reason that we can declare
For thinking a plain beefsteak, if well done,
Less good for supper than grill'd paws of bear.
But man's pall'd appetite his inclination
Impels to range beyond the bound precise
Of what he needs for simple sustentation :
And to the victims of his gourmandise
Simplicius felt a forcible temptation
To add (since new they were, and might be nice)
Grill'd paws of bear.   Just as no strange intrigue,
That to the list of all his old damnations
Added a new seduction, could fatigue
Don Juan in his search of fresh sensations.
So, for the sole dish of his lonely mess table,
Simplicius order'd *bear's paws*, to replenish
The stock of his experiences digestible,
And wash'd them down with half a flask of Rhenish.
The dish he chose was perfectly detestable ;
But still his stomach did not prove rebellious,
For fancy flatter'd him that he had fed
On food which might have tempted a Vitellius.
In which benign belief he went to bed.

5.

Near morn he dream'd a dream.   He dream'd his Bear
Was turn'd into a Lady, tall and stately :

And dream'd that he, himself, her fingers fair
With fervour kiss'd. Then, as she smiled sedately,
He sigh'd " Ah madam ! if you could but tell
How charming, grill'd with Tartar sauce, it is,
Before the altar, with your heart as well,
You would on me bestow the hand I kiss !"
His sleep was broken by the Postboy's horn
Just as the fair dame of his dream replied
Blushing, and like a lady nobly born
Whose passion struggles with a modest pride,
" Ah Baron, libertines such flatterers are !
And trustful fools are we. Unhand me, pray !
There's nothing in the world that can compare
With dog, served up in honey, the new way."

6.

The sun was beaming brightly thro' the casement,
Mine host had brought the coffee. From repose,
Still half between amusement and amazement,
Simplicius, smiling at his dream, arose :
Finish'd his breakfast : lighted his cigar :
And sprang into his carriage, quite elate.
He knew his own good mansion was not far.
A few hours brought him to the castle gate.

7.

He cross'd the court, surprised and somewhat sadden'd
That Nero, faithful guardian of his hall,

With no gay bark his silent entry gladden'd.
Nor came the good dog to his master's call.
But more, anon, that master's heart was grieved
When, to him coming o'er the cloister'd flags,
His agèd Major Domo he perceived
With palsied head bound up in bloody rags.
And " Ah my lord," the old man cried, "alas !
Alas, and woe the day !"--" Why, honest Andrew,
Why such affliction ?   What hath come to pass ? "
Only a heavy sigh that agèd man drew.
" What mean those bloody bandages ? " — " Dear
    master,"
The old man whimper'd with a whine of woe,
" My hair's clean gone in that accurst disaster,
And to my grave I in a wig must go."

8.

" Man, what disaster ? "—" O, the Bird, the Bird ! "
" What bird? and what has happen'd? tell me what ? "
Simplicius cried by sad forebodings stirr'd,
" And O the Cat," groan'd Andrew, " O the Cat ! "
Then on he rambled, all ejaculation,
" O, my good master ! O, my hair ! my hair !
And O, the Dog ! "   With rising agitation
" The dog ? " exclaim'd Simplicius.   " And the Bear,
The Bear ! " groan'd Andrew.   " What a situation ! "
" Quick ! " cried his master, "all the truth declare."
Then, drop by drop as 'twere, this sad narration
Oozed from the depths of the old man's despair.

9.

Andrew, the moment that his lord was gone,
Had yielded to a wish long while represt,
A wild emotion ever and anon
Haunting good servants—to disturb their rest,
And, more, their master's. For so fine a border
Between extremes is in this planet scurvy,
That when they want to set the house in order
Your servants always turn it topsy-turvy.
The house, in this case, was the bird's house merely ;
But much the bird disliked that innovation.
And we ourselves, who have experienced yearly
The same conditions, and the same sensation,
Can understand the bird's bewilder'd rage.
Retreating rest'essly, without success,
From one nook to another of his cage,
He tried to escape that demon, Cleanliness ;
And at the last, his incommoded premises
Deserting altogether, forth he flew.
But that desertion the avenging Nemesis
Of violated custom did pursue.
Infatuating freedom more and more
Confused his soul, already in confusion ;
And now against the ceiling, now the floor,
He flounced with flop, and flutter, and contusion ;
Flew bounce against the cornice of the door,
Then, clamorous, at the casement's cold delusion
Which mock'd him (since for him they waved no
    more)

With sight of waving woods in wild profusion.
At length he turn'd to books for consolation,
And o'er the bookcase perch'd in Gothic gloom.
Andrew, bewilder'd too, took that occasion
To hasten to the pantry for a broom.
But when, with this new engine of persuasion,
He to the chase return'd,—alas o'erpowering
(As well it might be) was his consternation
To find the Cat (more quick than he) devouring
The last few bloody feathers of the Bird.

10.

"Beast!" cried Simplicius, when the story came
To this sad point, and by resentment stirr'd
He rose in haste, "I'll bring her to the scratch!"
"Alas, my lord," old Andrew cried with shame,
"That's what I tried. But cats are hard to catch.
I hurl'd my broomstick, like a javelin, at her:
She thro' the door, left open, darted: hard
Behind her, down the stairs with cry and clatter,
I after: and so out across the yard.
This Nero saw: and judged the Cat in fault.
Nor judged he wrong. The little murderess fled;
But Nero (honest dog) still barking 'halt'
Fleet on her sly and felon footsteps sped.
Poor Puss! . . . He meant it for the best .
        and yet——
'Twixt dog and cat there's ancient feud 'tis said,
Like that between my lords of Capulet

And Montague, of which in books I've read.
But I'll believe not that our Nero's breast
Lodged hate like theirs—or any hate at all.
Too good was he ! He meant it for the best.
The Cat had sprung upon the Bear-pit's wall.
The Dog sprang after.   With a gallant grip
He pinn'd her by the throat, and . . . squeak!"——
              " The brute !"
Simplicius cried, " but he shall feel my whip.
Go, fetch it !"   Andrew, melancholy mute,
Turn'd, brush'd his hand across his eyes, and said
" Nero will never feel the whip again."

                    11.

The old man sigh'd profoundly, shook his head,
And then resumed.   " Regrets and threats are vain.
O what a sight ! methinks I see it yet.
The Cat was down.   The Dog above her stood.
But both were struggling on the parapet.
The Cat's white coat was red with clots of blood,
With blood the Dog's black muzzle.   And meanwhile,
Perch'd on his pole, the Bear this conflict eyed ;
Smiling, as well as such a brute can smile,
And wagg'd his hideous head from side to side.
His paws, with an atrocious affectation,
Cross'd loose and languid o'er his bulky breast,
His small eyes, all unwonted animation,
Glowing expectant with a greedy zest.
And all this time the monster humm'd with pleasure,

And all this time the moment's helpless dread
Crippled me like a paralytic seizure.
The Cat, at last, lay still.   I deem'd her dead.
Is there a second Cat-world, as I'm fain
To hope, where cats redeem'd, without relapse,
By birds untempted, and by dogs unslain,
Live and do better ?   Pardon'd there, perhaps.
Each sinful puss may yet to peace attain.
Else why earth's torturing trials, dogs, guns, traps ?
Whilst thus I mused, up sprang the Cat again,
And dealt the Dog a buffet in the chaps.
That was her dying effort.   In surprise
The Dog set up a howl—recoil'd—slipp'd—fell
Into the pit—I turn'd away mine eyes,
And what I could not see I cannot tell.
It overcomes me.   Never to that wall
My looks are turn'd without a pang of pain.
He was a dog who, take him all in all,
We shall not look upon his like again."

12.

And, since the old man's utterance fail'd him, here
Stepp'd, cap in hand, the Keeper from the clan
Of listening servants who had gather'd near,
And " Save your lordship's presence," he began,
" 'Tis too much for the old one.   Let him be.
More bravely then, my lord, himself he bore.
Three skips into the house to find the key,
And down the stairs again in three skips more.

Next moment in old Bruin's den was he.
Ay, without fear ! without his hat, too.   Well,
Meanwhile there rested nothing but a ruin
Of broken bones to mark where Nero fell,
And these the Bear was mumbling.   ' Bruin ! Bruin !
Bruin, you brute !' cried Andrew.   Bruin stopp'd
Mouthing the mangled morsels of poor Nero
Which leisurely with surly calm he dropp'd,
And Lord ! my heart sank in me down to zero
When I beheld him on his hind legs stalking
(As proud as any Christian, please your lordship)
And, with a growl of beastly rage, half walking
Half reeling, as we landsmen do aboard ship,
Up to the old one."—" Shoot him !" groan'd Simplicius.
The Keeper nodded, " That's already done.
For I was there.   I knew the brute was vicious,
And with me, by good luck, I had my gun.
'Twas plaguy hard to aim, tho', 'twixt the pair o' them,
Bruin's black waistcoat, Master Andrew's blue one—
Hard to see which the man, and which the bear, o'
        them—
Half hid by both, one small white spot—the true one—
No bigger than a button.   Well, I cover—
Fire—and three fall—Andrew, the Bear, and I.
Ay, ay ! 'twas not my gun that kick'd me over.
My heart went thump, and that I'll not deny.
When I came round, my wife says, like a dumb thing
I stared about, and whiter than a cheese.
Good reason, too ! I knew I had kill'd something,
The Bear or Andrew—one, or both of these.

'Twas Andrew luckily—I mean, 'twas he
My shot had saved.   The Bear was dead as mutton.
My ball was in him just where it should be,
In that white spot no bigger than a button.

13.

" Ay, dead and done !   But 'faith ! in his last jigs
He scalp'd the old one clean as Indians do ;
And that's why Andrew talks of wearing wigs,
Forgetting he was bald ten years ago.
But since that day the old one's just" . . . And here
The keeper slowly lifted to his forehead
A furtive finger.   Lost in musings drear
" Ah," sigh'd Simplicius, " it is all too horrid !"
Then, with a vacant dreamy air, as one
Whose thoughts are vext by the interposition
Of some vague memory that's come and gone
Before it finds within him recognition,
" What with the carcass of the Bear was done?"

14.

The Keeper answer'd " With my lord's permission,
' A badger's half a sort of bear,' said I.
The badger is the Keeper's perquisite,
And, deeming thus the Bear mine own, for why?
I shot him, nor could bear be better hit,
I skinn'd the beast.   His grease I melted down.
The barbers bought it.   For next winter's cold

His fur I kept. And in the market town
His venison to a poulterer I sold."
" Heavens !" groan'd Simplicius, and against his brow
He struck his fist. For now the truth flash'd clear,
And he remorsefully remember'd how
He had eaten his own bear's paws at THE BEAR.

15.

The Cat had eaten up the Bird : ere she
In turn, a victim, to the Dog had pass'd.
The Bear had feasted on the Dog : and he,
Horror, had feasted on the Bear at last !
Thus he who, for their orgies too carnivorous,
Against Cat, Dog, and Bear had just protested
Was proved (from such injustice Saints deliver us !)
To have both eaten, relish'd, and digested
The Bear, and, with the Bear, the Bear's own dinner,
Bird, Cat, and Dog, besides—vicarious sinner !

16.

He gazed around him with a rueful eye
That miss'd each loved and lately murder'd quality.
In fancy he beheld the Blackbird die ;
The Cat a victim to the Dog's brutality ;
The Dog devour'd by the Bear ; and by
Himself the Bear, with Roman sensuality
Of stomach *audax omnia perpeti !*
And, seeing too, no fancy but reality,
The scalp'd pate of his mangled Major Domo,
" *Fiat justitia,*" groan'd he, " *pereat homo !*"

XXX.

THE ROCK.

1.

For ages standing, still for ages stood
    (To stand and to withstand was all his care)
A Rock : whose feet were in the unfathom'd flood,
    His forehead in the illimitable air.
    Upon his brow the centuries beat,
        And left it, as they found it, bare ;
    The rolling waters round his feet
        Roll'd, and roll'd otherwhere.

2.

And those cold feet of his the fawning waves
    Lick'd, slave-like, ever with a furtive sigh ;
Save when at times they rose, and (still like slaves)
    In rebel scum, with insubordinate cry,
    Strove, and, tho' fiercely, strove in vain
        To drag down him that stood so high ;
    Then fell ; and at his feet again
        Fawn'd—with a furtive sigh.

3.

The Storm and he were brothers ; but in feud.
    One lived a station'd, one a wandering, life :
This to subdue, that to be unsubdued,
      Put forth his strength in unfraternal strife.
    The burden of one weary brother
      Was to resist, and to remain :
  A fiercer fate impell'd the other
      To strive, and strive in vain.

4.

A homeless wanderer over the wide world,
    A sullen spirit with a fleeting form,
That pass'd in soil'd and tumid mantle furl'd,
      For ever and for ever roam'd the Storm.
    But o'er the sea, with shoulders bent
      And backward scowl before the blast,
  He, flying, to his discontent
      Beheld the Rock stand fast ;

5.

And lingering hover'd, restless, round and round,
    To vex the rest that vex'd him.   But the Rock,
Beaten and buffeted, yet not uncrown'd,
      Stood, and withstood ; and sadly seem'd to mock
    The Force which cries from age to age
      In accent fierce " Give way !"

With that which, ignorant of rage,
    For ever answers " Nay ! "

6.

Then stoop'd the Storm, and whisper'd to the waves,
    " Are ye so many, and afraid of one ?
The world is yours, if ye but knew, poor slaves !
    Dare to be lords, and lo, the world is won ! "
To that wild tempter's whisper rose
        Their hundred heads, soon dasht in spray ;
    But these succeeding fast to those
        Renew'd the frustrate fray ;

7.

Until the Storm could lift the waves no higher ;
    Then, with a scornful sigh letting them fall,
And self-pursued by unappeased desire,
    He left them, as he found them, slaves.   And all
That strife without result for ever
        Ends only to begin again ;
    Subsiding but for fresh endeavour,
        Eternal, yet in vain.

8.

But, in the intervals of time, among
    The fissures of the Rock, have birds of prey
Built themselves nests : who, fishing for their young,
    Dive in the waves, and snatch the fish away.

And heaven its feather'd generations
    Renews to vex from year to year
The sea's folk, as their scaly nations
    Appear, and disappear.

9.

The fishes needs must suffer and endure,
    Unable to retaliate on the birds ;
And of their fishy wrongs which find no cure
    The wide-mouth'd fools complain in watery words,
    " Hath Providence for pasture given
      The weak for ever to the strong ?
    Is there no justice, then, in Heaven ?
      No sense of right and wrong ?"

10.

The Storm (that never leaves it long at rest)
    Return'd anon to trouble the still sea,
But that eternal revolutionist
    Seem'd to these short-lived sufferers to be
A young deliverer, waited long,
    Whom, in the fulness of late time,
Heaven raised to rectify the wrong,
    And punish prosperous crime.

11.

And when the devastating waves roll'd high,
    And drave the birds, and drench'd their dwellings
      thro',

The fishes cried, exulting, " Verily
  There *is* a judge that judgeth just and true !
The judgment day hath dawn'd at last :
  Now strikes the final judgment hour :
The future shall redeem the past,
  And lift the poor to power !"

12.

The Rock stood fast—tho' bare of nest and bird :
  The Storm was spent : the sunk sea ceased from
    striving,
And, in the stillness, that grey hermit heard
  This fuss of exultation and thanksgiving.
The water trickled from his wet
  Wave-ravaged crest, and dripp'd below,
As, after battle, drops the sweat
  Down from a hero's brow.

13.

" Is it for this," within him mused the strong
  And melancholy spirit of his life,
" For *this*, that I stand here — who knoweth how
    long,
  Who knoweth wherefore ?—in eternal strife !
And gaze into the nether deep
  And up to heaven's huge hollowness,
And, while the ages o'er me sweep,
  Question the void abyss,

14.

" Sad, yet supreme ; and weary, yet awake !
  And must I listen still, and still must hear,
How of a final judgment—for their sake—
    (*Their* sake, who but appear to disappear !)
    These sprats and sparrows gurgle and twitter ?"
      So mused the Rock ; his gray
    Bare summit redden'd by the glitter
      Of the departing day.

15.

And, whilst he mused, athwart the trembling plain
  His shade, unnoticed, sped with stealthy flight
Far on the dim horizon to attain
    The obscurely safe asylum of the night ;
    As tho', for once, unvext, unview'd,
      That Rock's soul fain would be
    From the eternal solitude
      Of his own greatness free.

16.

But greatness grants to greatness no escape.
  Fierce on the timorous vagrant's furtive track
The sudden sunrise flashing smote this shape
    Of baffled darkness to its birthplace back ;
    And there, where Splendour seem'd to mock
      Its slave whose flight was vain,
    Deep in his own brave heart the Rock
      Buried his shade again.

XXXI.

D E M O S.

.

PART I.

WHEN Light first dawn'd, to Chaos came repose :
    Shapes, from the sheeted shapelessness unfurl'd,
Took rank in order ranged : the Mountains rose,
    And found themselves the monarchs of the world.

The sunrise, bearing tribute, all night long
    Travell'd the globe, and brought them eastern gold
Daily at earliest dawn.   Bright breastplates strong
    The skill'd frost forged them of white-colour'd cold.
Round their firm thrones sharp lightnings flash'd like
        swords,
    And guarding thunders girt their crowns.   The plain
Bore, in fond homage to his highborn lords,
    The floating purple of their princely train.
Forest, to deck their pomp, with forest vied,
    Mantled, and clasp'd them round with emerald zones;

Whilst dainty lawns spread broider'd carpets wide
   O'er all the soft approaches to their thrones,
For easy kneeling.   Clouds, like stately cares
   That haunt the sombre foreheads of the great,
Burthen'd   their   brows.   But   eagles,   too,   were
     theirs,
   That eyed the sun undazzled, and elate
As bold ambitions in imperial minds.
   To earth's far frontiers, bearing banner'd shower
And blowing solemn trump, the wingèd winds,
   Their wandering heralds, did proclaim their power.
The fertile rivers, and fresh streams, were fed
   On the rich bounty of their royal grace.
Each rebel billow at their feet fell dead.
   They were creation's crown'd and sceptred race.

But, scorn'd, obscure, down trampled in the dirt
   And miry drench of their dark hollows, lay
Unable to uplift himself—inert,
   And lacking noble form—the lumpish Clay.
And to himself the Clay said " Trodden down,
   Here in abasement must I bear their scorn
Who, glittering with a glory not their own,
   Boast of the accident of being born
In lofty station ?   Fashion'd were we both
   Of the same substance, gender'd from the womb
Of the same mother ; and shall theirs, forsooth,
   Be all the glory, and all mine the gloom ?
'Twere better not to be, than to be thus,
   Earth's common footstool.   Better not to live

Than to live under lorddom tyrannous,
   Strong to endure, but impotent to strive !
Yet must I hide me, and my wrongs, away,
   Till strike mine hour.   And strike it will.   Mean-
      while,
Patience, be thou my prophet ! "   And the Clay
   Slunk from the sun's unsympathising smile,
And roll'd himself into the river's bed,
   And there lay hidden.

                  Time pass'd.   Man appear'd,
And laid his hand on Nature.   For his bread
   The glebe was harrow'd, and the forest clear'd.
He turn'd, and tamed, the torrent to his will :
   Bridged the broad river, fell'd the flourishing oak :
Groped in the granite bowels of the hill
   For hidden ore : and rent with flame and smoke
The ribs of royal mountains.   Down they came,
   Shorn by the saw, and measured by the rod,
To build man's palaces, and bear his name
   Carved in their flesh.   The earth had a new god.

PART II.

Large was the chamber ; bathed with light serene
   And silence tuned, not troubled, by the sound
Of one cool fountain tinkling in the green
   Of laurel groves that girt the porches round.

And in that chamber the sole dwellers were
　　Ideas, clad in clear and stately shape ;
Save one, a prisoner, huge, uncouth, and bare,
　　Hung fast in fetters, hopeless of escape,
And broken at the heart,—a Marble Block.
　　Even as a hero, in base ambuscade
Fallen ; so, fall'n, and from his native rock
　　Borne here in chains, the indignant Marble made
No moan ; but round, in dumb remonstrance gazed ;
　　And, gazing, saw, surprised, all round him stand
The images of gods.　With right arm raised,
　　Jove launch'd the thunders from his loaded hand :
A light of undulating lovelinesses,
　　Rose foam-born Venus from the foam : and, dread
With dismal beauty, by its serpent tresses
　　Did sworded Perseus lift Medusa's head :
There paused a-tiptoe wing-capp'd Mercury :
　　Apollo, pensive smiling, linger'd here :
There stately Pallas stood, with brooding eye,
　　Full arm'd, and grasp'd the ægis and the spear.

A kindred instinct flash'd, a sudden glow
　　Thrill'd, sparkling, through the Marble's crystal
　　　grain.
" Flesh of my flesh," he cried, " I know you now,
　　You stately statues ! and myself would fain
Be also even as ye are."—" After me ! "
　　A mocking voice made answer from below.
" Wretch !" laugh'd the lucid Marble, " after *thee* ? "
　　For, not far off, he noticed, by a row

Of pitchers, huddled in a slimy trough,
  The lumpish Clay.   "Baseborn, how darest thou
    show
Thy face in Beauty's sanctuary ?   Off !
  Did not I banish thee when I" . . . "When thou
Thyself wast yet unbanisht, wouldst thou say ?
  True ! in thy pride thou couldst not then foresee
The hour when *me* thou must perforce obey.
  For thou *wilt* have to obey me."—"Obey *thee* ?"
" Ay ! grinding thy gnasht teeth against the fine
  Keen flitting chisel, when thy nature stern
Must needs submit to serve each fluent line
  My form imposes on it ; that, in turn,
Thou mayst, by following me, be something."—"I !
  I follow *thee*, wretch ?"—" Ho ! not broken yet
Is thy proud spirit ? Patience ! By and by
  Thou, too, wilt need, as I have needed, it."

PART III.

The Artist strode into the statued hall,
  Up to the block ; and, with pleased eyes perused
The Marble's snowy sides, slow measuring all
    The length and breadth of them.   The while he
      mused,
Into the stone, with such intense regard,
  His deep gaze dived, that in a mystic thrill
It felt his human eye, throughout its hard
  And frozen bulk, with a creative will

Awakening beauteous forms in slumber claspt,
 Which heaved as tho' that will they half fore-
  knew.
Sudden, he stretch'd his searching hand, and
  grasp'd . . .
 —Ah strange! 'Twas not the Chisel that now flew
Dartlike, obedient to that aiming eye,
 Into the heart of the expectant stone.
His Thought plunged, kneading, in the trough hard by,
 And clods of viscous Clay, one after one,
Thick on the table thump'd with clumsy thud :
 There, grew together : wormlike writhing, rose
Pliant to every touch : until the mud,
 Gliding and glutinous, 'gan half disclose
The thought that quicken'd it. Its impish speed
 Was half, like Caliban, ungainly, half,
Like Ariel, delicate, till Fancy freed
 Her image struggling from it. With low laugh
" Seest thou ? " it lisp'd and mutter'd. " Seest thou ?
  Try
 To follow *me* now ; and mine image take
Upon thee. Which of us hath (I or thou)
 The fine creative faculty to make
Ideas first corporeal ? " And, complete
 In clay, a statue stood before the gaze
Of the astonisht Marble.
    Then, to eat
 Slowly, and gnaw through all the intricate maze
Of netted lines about his body thrown,
 The griding chisel, with three-corner'd wedge,

Ground his keen tooth upon the spluttering stone
   Which sprang and split in sparkles round the edge,
Driven by the dancing mallet.   By degrees
   The out-thrust throat and formidable face
Assume imperative purpose : fingers seize
   And grasp the fluttering scroll with eager grace :
The deep eye darkens under beetling brows :
   The half-uplifted arm begins to shake
The toga's massive fold, that backward flows:
   And the stretcht finger points.   What words awake
Upon those quivering lips?   What thunder-speech
   Upheaves the fierce Democracy, and breaks
The power of pale Patricians cowering each
      From that curl'd lip?   For lo, THE TRIBUNE
        speaks!
The Tribune?   O proud Marble, royal born,
   Thou the coarse organ of the Demos? thou !
" Art thou enough humiliated, Scorn?
   Pride, is thy loftiness at last brought low ? "
The base material, to the nobler one
   Form'd after its own image, sneer'd.   " By Me,
And after me !   'Tis thus, and thus alone,
   That, proud one, thou henceforth hast leave to be."

But the pure Marble, in the image clothed
   Of a new power, still conscious to the last
Of all his ancient force, made answer " Loathed
   Abortive botch !   A granted garb thou hast,
But think not thou art safe in it.   ' By thee?'
   Through thee, say rather : who hast now made known

Undream'd of means, and mightier ones, to me
   Of being above thee.   Look, fool, on thine own
Futile and perishable frame.   Behold !
   Already runs the gaping fissure straight
From head to heel.   For all thy boasting bold,
   Thy tottering limbs can scarce support the weight
Of thy flaw'd body ; and thy flimsy flesh
   Hastily put together, may not long
Uphold thy silly head.   Some crevice fresh
   Is daily widening those loose clods among.
Drunk with the fancied triumph of a day,
   Thou staggerest.   Me, superior still, thou must
Invoke to represent thee.   Baseborn Clay,
   Slave of the immortal Marble, sink—in dust !"

XXXII.

A PROMETHEUS UNBOUND.

"Ich unglücksel'ger Atlas!" — HEINRICH HEINE.*

'Twas the lot of a cork in a bottle,
    (Who, bound with wire, and wound with twine,
Was a prisoner himself, held fast by the throttle)
    To imprison a generous wine.
And oh, proud, how proud of his lot was he,
The oppressor of that strong spirit to be !
But alas for the chances of power,
    And the ups and dows of a ruler's life !
For once, in a festal hour,
    Somebody suddenly seizing a knife,
(This happen'd on board of a ship at sea)
    Cut asunder the bonds which till then had held fast
    That cork to his boasted place.   Then at last
The fiery force in the flask, set free
And upshooting a foamy fountain, tost
    The bung from the bottle, and overboard.

* Me miserable Atlas !

And thus was his proud supremacy lost,
  When sustain'd no longer by steel and cord.

" Revolution !" that was the cork's first word,
  As splash ! he fell on his flimsy pate.
" Such another the universe never will see.
  What a greatness there is in the fall of the great !
O what an uprising—and all against *me !*
And, ye gods ! what a strength was mine, so long
To have held in subjection a spirit so strong ! "
Whilst thus he was speaking, o'er him descended
  (Taking him suddenly captive again)
A broken kettle, too bad to be mended,
  Which the ship's cook happen'd to pitch just then
Out of the cabin-window.   It fell
Inclosing the cork like a diving-bell ;
And souse, together both cork and can
Sunk to the bed of the ocean.
There, in the dismal abyss, through chasms
  Of the scoriac crust of the dædal earth,
The central fire with volcanic spasms
  Was hurling upward in monstrous mirth
Mighty masses of burning stone.
" Thou, too, O Earth," cried the cork with a groan,
" Art overwhelm'd by rebellious powers
Jealous of majesty mighty as ours !
  Well, such is the fate, as it seems of the great
In these bad times, my Royal Brother !
  There is something wrong in the universe.
  I myself, as thou seest, have suffer'd reverse.
One fallen grandeur can feel for another."

Meanwhile, that irruption submarine
Was belching granite into the brine;
And the split stones, tumbling heavy and hot,
Buried beneath them cork and pot.
The former his inborn levity,
    And natural disposition to keep
On the surface (being restrain'd thereby)
    Made ill at ease in his dungeon deep.
And he said, with a self-compassionate sigh,
" The last of the Titan race am I,
Titanic sufferer!   Envious Fate,
Of how heavy a world of woes thy hate,
Hath made me Atlas!"   That dark Power
Whose unseen finger fashions the hour,
And guides blind Chance to her destined work,
Heard this complaint of the querulous cork;
And, smiling a secret smile of contempt,
    Scatter'd the stones that imprison'd him :
Who, as soon as he found himself thus exempt
    From external pressure, up thro' the dim
Vague and voluminous element
Wavering back to the surface went.

There did the light-headed loiterer roll
From ripple to ripple, without a goal ;
Vacant of power and purpose too ;
Drifting, shifting, with nothing in view.
Hither and thither the waters drew him :
This way, that way, the breezes blew him :
Fishes snapp'd at him now and then,
Half-swallow'd and spat him out again :

Whilst, restored to his own inherent want
Of stability, ever he lightly glided
(As wave and wind were predominant)
On the course by his chance—not choice—decided.

O Atlas ! what of thy Titan doom,
Thine ocean-shroud, and thy mountain-tomb ?
Flimsy fragment of fungus stuff,
Too flimsy to perish, drift on still !
For in thee is not even weight enough
To dive, and be drown'd, of thine own free will.

XXXIII.

VALOUR.

1.

For free discussion of affairs of state
  The Beasts a public meeting held : and there
'Twas sad to hear how things had lapsed of late
  From bad to worse, and so degenerate were
That now the greatest rascals were the great.
  In fact the talk was such as everywhere,
Is heard at public meetings nowadays,
Where those who give most censure get most praise.

2.

An Ape, much cheer'd (he chatter'd like a man)
  Denounced the weakness of the government.
" Where shall we find true valour ?" he began.
  " Not in the craven crew we are content
To call our leaders.   Let him lead who can !
  Old kingdoms tempt new conquerors.   Prevent
The impending ruin of this empire old !
Tho' big, the brutes that lead us are not bold.

3.

" Or only bold to weaker beasts are they.
 There is not one of them (and that they know)
Who never yet was forced to slink away,
 Avoiding fight with some superior foe.
But as for that, what need of leaders, pray?
 Since turning tail's a trick we all can do.
True Valour flies not, tho' the foe be strong,
Nor works, by force or fraud, another's wrong;

4.

" True Valour neither seeks nor shuns to fight.
 Be his the royal crown, and his alone,
In whom true Valour doth those gifts unite
 Which guard a nation and endear a throne!"
The meeting would have echo'd with delight
 The Ape's discourse if, ere the Ape was done,
The Lion had not suddenly appear'd;
Whose presence was impressive, tho' uncheer'd.

5.

He rose, and round him roll'd a regnant eye;
 Calmly contemptuous was his ample brow;
And " What is it ye want?" he said. " If I,
 The Lion, be not valorous enow,
Where's he, so valorous, that he dares defy
 My power, forsooth unprized, I fain would know?

Is not my presence fear'd by those ye fear?
What more protection need ye?   I am here.

6.

" Peace, babbling mouths !   Not mine the fault, but
    theirs,
    If, trusting neither in themselves nor me,
Those poor poltroons, quails, pigeons, rabbits, hares,
    In panic flight too soon from danger flee.
The foe that slays the coward unawares
    Is his own coward heart's timidity.
Whose presence have I ever shunn'd? or who
Hath seen me shrink, or" . . . " Cock-a-doodle-do!"

7.

And " Doodle-do !" again the red Cock cried.*
    The Lion, with disgust beyond control,
Shrugg'd his huge mane—shrank—falter'd—turn'd
    aside,
    That vulgar voice, impertinently droll,
Offensive to his taste as to his pride,
    Set smarting in his sensitive strong soul
A secret nerve that found there no defence
From the coarse touch of clumsy insolence.

    * It is an old popular belief that the lion cannot bear the
crow of the cock. Schiller alludes to it in his Wallensteins
Lager. The sergeant says of the great Friedlander—
        " . . . When the cock crows he starts thereat."
To which the Jäger replies—
            He's one and the same with the lion in that."

8.

"There goes the bravest of the brave ! put out,
  Crow'd down !" the bald Ape jabber'd to the crowd.
The Bull, scarce knowing what 'twas all about,
  With sullen stare half stupid and half proud
Had seen the dunghill bird, and heard him shout,
  Heedless : but, while the hubbub wax'd more loud,
Close in the ear of him a crafty Crow
Cried, " Seize the moment, ere the moment go !

9.

" The throne is vacant. Claim and take it, thou !
  Address the people !" urged the black-robed bird.
" Or let me be thine orator. I know
  The habits and the humours of the Herd."
Then round the field he flew ; to high and low
  Persuasive spake, and counsell'd all who heard
To choose a bovine king. " For see," he said,
" What simple tastes, and what a solid head !

10.

" Mark, too, how great a following is his !
  Whose Party follows him where'er he goes.
What confidence ! and how deserved it is !
  On party strength well-balanced States repose.
And how respectable a party this !
  Republics only ripen public woes

To fatten despots. But can aught surpass
Sound Bourgeois Rule, with bellyfuls of grass?"

11.

These words the opinion of the public win.
   The cautious Stag, persuaded, plumps his vote :
The Stallion's high-bred ear at once takes in
   What takes in *him* too : the gregarious Goat
And ruminating Ram their numerous kin
   Lead to the poll ; and each loud-bleating throat
Proclaims invested with supreme authority
The Bull, by right of popular majority.

12.

The Fox mark'd this with ill-contented mind.
   He and the Crow are rivals in their trade ;
Attorneys both of pettifogging kind.
   Hovering about the Herd, the Crow hath made
From what its foolish followers drop behind
   A pretty profit ; by no means afraid
To pick from nastiness appropriate food.
Nothing's too nasty to do some one good.

13.

Quite otherwise is Lawyer Reynard's way.
   Respectable and prosperous corporations
He hates and shuns ; seeks geese that go astray ;
   Haunts backyards favouring nightly visitations ;

Estates ill-managed, fortunes in decay,
  These are his interests, these his occupations.
Sound bourgeois rule he cannot bear at all :
Reynard's romantic and a radical.

14.

"Fine doings!" mused he, "curse that prattling Crow !
  A sovereign ox, with corvine ministers ?
Not yet, good people, are we sunk so low
  If I can help it ! Patience, civic sirs !
Better the Lion ! He at least knew how
  To treat affairs as only grand seigneurs
Are able,—on a large and liberal scale,
Not stooping to contemptible detail.

15.

" He knew the world, and took it as it is,
  Nor ask'd five legs of mutton from a sheep.
Unpinn'd to prim respectabilities,
  Thro' many an awkward case he's let me creep,
And stopp'd the cackle of accusing geese ;
  Quashing the trial with a sovran sweep
Of his capacious and imperial paw.
A king was he, whose kingly word was law !

16.

" Nor cared he for a wee mouse more or less.
  In battle, we shall ne'er behold his peer.

He wanted parliamentary address,
  And that's a pity ; could not bear, 'tis clear,
The slightest interruption. Who would guess
  The voice of any vulgar chanticleer
Could crow him down ? Well, he and I were
    cronies,
But *his* day's done now. *Fuimus leones !*

17.

" As for the Bull, well know I where to find
  The heel of that Achilles ! Wait awhile,
And then you'll see the dance begin ! What kind
  Of cant is this that fills my veins with bile,
Of royal power with civic rights combined ?
  Preach it to fleas, and bugs, and such *canaille !*
True Valour claims no corporation-clause,
But stands complete upon its own four paws."

18.

Thus musing, Master Reynard slipp'd away
  By devious by-paths to a secret lair
Where many a plot he had been wont to lay.
  There now the rascal crouch'd and sniff'd the air
Till what he sought he found ;—a certain gay
  And greedy Gadfly, buzzing here and there
About a heap of carrion slyly stow'd
By paws felonious in that dark abode.

19.

" 'Tis well to have a friend in every class,
  And now and then be civil to small fry,"
The rogue laugh'd, lolling in the long dry grass ;
  And, having whisper'd to her, watch'd the Fly
With zealous hum about his business pass.
  Then, sure of the result, indifferently
He saunter'd after to the grazing ground.
And, like a casual lounger, look'd around.

20.

The Crow, meanwhile, with a triumphant caw,
  Was leading up the loyal deputation
Charged to present the crown, expound the law,
  And hail the elected monarch of the nation.
The Bull, with unconcern his subjects saw,
  But, graciously accepting their ovation,
Stoop'd, to receive the crown, his stolid head ;
When lo ! he shook, he shrank, he turn'd, he fled.

21.

He fled ! his eye, bewilder'd, sought all round
  Some unseen formidable foe : he fled
Just in the crowning moment : fled uncrown'd :
  Without the least word of dismissal said
To his amazed admirers. On the ground
  Stamping, and butting with an aimless head,

Off scamper'd, with him, all his Party too.
Tho' why, or where, not one of them quite knew.

22.

" There goes the second of the Sons of Fame ! "
    The scall'd Ape snicker'd to the gaping crowd.
" Did not I tell you? they are all the same !
    Like this Goliath by a Gadfly cow'd,
A swarm of Bees Sir Bruin overcame.
    Each hath his master, look he ne'er so proud.
Again I ask—look round you left and right,
Where is the chief incapable of flight ? "

23.

" I know the chief that never fled ; and know,
    Where now he dwells, the bravest of the brave ! "
This voice came, sudden, from a wither'd bough
    Where perch'd in pomp a Parrot grey and grave.
Much had he travell'd ; much with high and low
    Had mix'd ; and learn'd the world ; and seem'd to
        have
In every land where he had been a ranger
The world's respect : half citizen, half stranger.

24.

Seldom he spake.   Much given to thought he seem'd.
    No public office had he ever held ;

But, when he oped his beak, all listeners deem'd
    That they had heard an oracle of eld.
Sedate his mien; and all his language teem'd
    With sage enigmas : none its meaning spell'd :
All praised it more for that.   So judgments go.
Omne ignotum pro magnifico !

25.

Yet was this Parrot (the plain truth to own)
    At bottom an impostor, rake, and knave ;
Who in himself had selfishly lived down
    That love of freedom born in bosoms brave ;
Which he regarded as the cause and crown
    Of all the ills that mortal life enslave.
" For what's life worth," he thought, "if day by day
The worth of life wear life itself away ?

26.

" The tree that's not contented to be wood
    Doth all its strength to its own damage put,
In bringing forth what brings the tree no good ;
    Since others pluck the apple and the nut,
And each fool's toil but turns him into food
    For other mouths, whose greed its gettings glut.
Why plague one's soul, a plaguy world to please ?
Life's only fruit worth growing is life's ease.

27.

" *Per Bacco!*" (he had been in Italy)
"Give me the golden cage that I can quit
Whene'er I will because men know that I,
No fool, am sure to turn again to it!
Caramba!" (and in Spain) "where'er I fly
I find but folk that seem for Bedlam fit.
Oh, que les bêtes sont bêtes!" (and he had been
In France, where things worth seeing he had seen :

28.

Republics one and indivisible,
But more than one, and all divided ; ending
In master-strokes of state, whereby they fell ;
And empires that were peace, on war depending ;
And constitutions that for shot and shell
Were constituted marks, when past all mending ;
Cooks, captains, orators, mobs, proclamations,
And demi-worlds for demi-reputations).

29.

" *Oh, que les bêtes sont bêtes!* 'Tis pitiable !
Cannot they see how easily mankind
May be enslaved by any beast that's able,
With just a show of serving men, to bind
Men to its bestial service ? Stall and stable
Where cow and horse their cared-for comfort find,

What beast but man would build for horse and cow ?
Or in their service sweat his boasted brow ?

30.

" And all for what? a little milk from one ;
    Or leave the other's body to bestride,
Who in man's seeming service (which is none)
    Doth only what his pleasure 'tis, and pride,
To do when free—trot, gallop, leap, and run !
    For me, the fools a glittering house provide,
That's finer than their own, a dome of gold,
Because I call them bitter names, and scold !

31.

" *Cospetto !* and what brainless brutes be these
    Who seek a master simply to be free !
When they might get them, if they did but please,
    A servant, whose sole business it would be
To emancipate them from the miseries
    Of freedom ! " Perch'd upon his wither'd tree
Whilst thus the Parrot mused, the Beasts below him
Roar'd, " Lead us to our leader ! name him ! show
    him ! "

32.

" He ! " the grey mocker slowly made reply,
    " The bravest of the brave, whose name ye ask,

Retired he dwells, in that obscurity
    Which ofttimes wraps the unrequited task
True Merit ever is content to ply.
    For Fame is but a hollow-sounding mask
Which to the crowd reëchoes its own voice,
And thence comes praise or blame, by chance, not
        choice.

33

" Retired he dwells : remote, serene, alone :
    Firm as the far-off rock where he abides :
Calm, tho' around him stormy waters roll :
    No base ambition in his soul resides :
By force or fraud, he wrongs not any one :
    Yet never, never, whatsoe'er betides,
Doth flinch a hair's-breadth from the fiercest foe."
" Long live our leader !" roar'd the Beasts below.

34.

" His name ! his name !" The Parrot from the tree
    Perch'd on whose blighted bough he sat sedate
With curious scrutiny observed the glee
    Of those beneath him ; slowly scratch'd his pate ;
Rough'd all his feathers ; seemed, awhile, to be
    O'erwhelm'd in thought profound, deliberate
As one who weighs each word against objection ;
Then answer'd, with emphatic circumspection.

35.

" Are ye resolved (think once and twice again !)
    To test true valour by the trial set
To those whose vaunted valour ye disdain,
    And hold him bravest of the brave, who yet
By force, or fraud, hath never spoil'd, or slain,
    Another ; but whom never foeman, met
In fiercest fight, hath ever forced to flee ?"
" Speak to the point !" the crowd cried.   " Who is
        he ?

36.

" Name him ! where is he ? question us no more !
    'Tis thee we question.   Give us plain replies.
He, only he, is worthy to reign o'er
    Those who to Valour have decreed the prize !"
The rest was one enthusiastic roar.
    A twinkle glitter'd in the wily eyes
Of that grey trifler, whilst for prudent flight
He spread his wings, and scream'd, with grim delight,

37.

" Ridiculous and cowardly *canaille !*
    Who jeer and flout the fine infirmities
Of noble minds ! whose natures mean and vile
    The Lion's courage, the Bull's strength despise,
And sneer at all ye cannot reconcile
    With trite decorums ! who can claim your prize ?
No creature ever known to run or royster.
Ye bid me name your chief ?   I name the Oyster !"

XXXIV.

PAIN.

1.

Satan, the Prince of Pain, whose rebel wing
    Creation cages under golden bars,
Wander'd his world-wide penthouse, hovering
    Among the mazy courses of the stars,
And mock'd the music of the spheres : " Beat time
    To the dull march of Matter's doom'd routine,
    Mechanics of Creation ! ye are mine,
Tho' me you praise not with your patient chime."

2.

Fierce cries of anguish mixt with shouts of mirth
    Rose as he spake.   The Rebel Angel laugh'd
" I know that music.   'Tis the babbling Earth
    Still to mine ears the self-same song doth waft.
Old is each note of it.   Complaints and curses !
    Murder and robbery in all forms of life,
    And dust, for dust, with dust in endless strife ;
Princes for provinces, and pads for purses !

3.

" Creatures of crocodile-creating clay,
　　Think ye your croaking, or your crunching, worth
Satanic intervention?　Have your way,
　　You self-made victims of the vulgar Earth !
But long live Love, in whose light air-balloon
　　　　Faith soars to heaven, self-confident and vain,
　　　　And falls with broken limbs to earth again,
Cursing her madcap voyage to the moon !

4.

" The good old classic music !　Passion quench'd
　　In hissing tears.　Fond greed of fancied gain
That sinks in sight of port.　The fist fierce-clench'd
　　That strikes the despot brow it served in vain.
Thought's shamed confession ' Unattainable !'
　　　　Affection's lamentation ' Lost !'　Hope's moan
　　　　' Defeated !'　Effort's deathcry ' Overthrown !'
Well done, ye faithful servitors of Hell !

5.

" I recognise your work, and give it praise."
　　And the Dark Spirit smiled.　But suddenly
Was wafted to him, from within that maze
　　Of miserable sounds, a single sigh ;
So faint, it scarce divided the vext air
　　　　More than a silence ; yet of such strange pain

As waked the past in Satan's soul again,
And thrill'd with memory his immense despair.

6.

He, spreading sullen pinions, earthward bent
  Swift flight; to find the archer whose strong bow
The torment of its venom'd shaft had sent
  Into such endless distances of woe.
There, scarce perceptible, the Fiend perceived
  A little saucy Imp, whose fingers fine
  Held with affected languor feminine
A bunch of fresh-blown roses, dewy-leaved.

7.

And from this posy now and then he took
  A single rose; and with a playful smile
Leaflet from leaflet lightly loosening, shook
  The petals o'er a wretch who all the while
Writhed under each in agony. That small
  Tormentor seem'd to sniff with keen delight
  Some gust of suffering made more exquisite
By every fragrant rose-leaf he let fall.

8.

" 'Twas thou then?"—" Mighty Master, it was I."
  " What new atrocity of torturing
Hast thou invented, Imp of Hell? That sigh
  Which made me shudder, even me thy king,

How hast thou wrung it from a human heart?
　What was thy weapon? scorpions seethed in flame?
　Or fangs of adders?　Name me, Imp, its name,
And show me how 'tis shaped, thy devilish dart."

9.

The little plump-cheek'd cherub of the pit
　(A kid among the goats, with budding horn)
Falter'd—"Dread Lord, I know no name for it.
　Soft are my roses, and without a thorn."
"Why thus, then, dost thou strew them?"—"Pardon
　　me,"
　　The Hell-whelp whined, "this man hath suffer'd
　　so!"
　　"Ha, fool! and thou dost pity him?　Go, go,
And learn mankind.　Thou art a child, I see."

10.

Blushing resentful, "Prince," the Imp replied,
　"What dost thou take me for?　'Tis true my bro-
　　thers
Are bigger, but" (and this he lisp'd with pride)
　"I scorn their clumsy practice.　How those others
Fatigue themselves in torturing mankind,
　　Get out of breath in running down their prey! |
　　My work, if easier, is more refined,
Look at this wretch's wounds.　How fresh are they!

11.

" From men he got them, Master, not from me.
    Yet each hath been a master-stroke I swear.
Which, but that *one by one* he got them, he
    Had surely not had strength enough to bear.
Man's work, yet perfect ! Hate without remorse :
        Deep thought : deliberate purpose : patient skill :
        Oh, naught was wanting to each human will
That stabb'd here ! How could this man's wounds be
    worse ?

12.

" I merely keep them open. Toucht again,
    Tho' ne'er so lightly, each one burns and gapes.
A rose-leaf does it. By disguised disdain
    That friendship's frank commiseration apes,
Men taught me this. The trick is simple, see !
        Yet 'neath such touches strongest spirits wince."
        " Away ! away ! " cried Hell's impatient Prince ;
" Release yon sufferer, leave his soul to me."

13.

The chidden Imp, reluctant, left his prey,
    Like a chased fly. Man's arch accuser stood
Contemplating man's victim. Silent lay
    The wretch, unconscious of worse neighbourhood
Than he had felt before. In that soul's curse
        The gaze of Satan, piercing, could detect

How heart and brain met shatter'd to reflect
In a flaw'd mirror a warp'd universe.

14.

" And thou hast suffer'd greatly ? " musing said
   The Prince of Pain. The sufferer slowly raised
The heavy burthen of a hopeless head,
   And, 'neath a half-uplifted eyelid, gazed
Upon the Rebel Angel's ruin'd brow,
     And recognised Hell's Anarch, and replied
     Indifferently, with neither shame nor pride,
Unto the voice of Satan, " Even as thou."

15.

" Then 'twas too much," mutter'd the Fiend. " I own
   No peer in torment; and I scorn to share
With human brows my solitary crown.
   Soul,—whom man's hate hath forced mine own to
     spare,
Lest at the last extremity his prey
     Should prove in aught my rival,—rest ! " And
     slow,
     With wistful gesture, from that human woe
Satan, half-sighing, turn'd, and fled away.

XXXV.

QUESTIONABLE CONSOLATION.

1.

A BUTTERFLY (and had the wretch been born
With all the beauties that, at best, adorn
  A butterfly's complete perfection, still
He but a butterfly had been, at best)
Came into life a cripple; dispossest
  Of half his natural features; born i' the chill,
Blemisht, and misbegotten; an abortion
Doom'd from the birth to suffering and distortion.

2.

One wing unfinisht, and misshapen one:
Six legs he had, but of his six legs none
  That served the purpose for which legs are made:
The piteous pivot of his own distress,
Aye with self-torturing unsteadiness
  About himself he turn'd; and found no aid
In aught that life vouchsafed him, leg or wing,
To life's attainment of one wisht-for thing.

3.

He saw the others hovering in the sun ;
He saw them seek each other ; saw them shun
    Each other, by each other to be sought ;
He saw them (each, itself, a second flower)
On flowers, entranced by the transcendent power
    Of their own happiness ; he saw them, fraught
With frolic rapture, fearless wantons all !
And saw himself, unable even to crawl.

4.

" And I," he thought, " I too, was meant to be
A wingèd joy, a wandering ecstasy !
    Ah, must I envy, for his happier lot,
The wingless worm that hath, complete, whate'er
As worm he wants ; who wants no more, to fare
    Thro' life content ; by life defrauded not
Of what mere life makes capable of joy
Even in a worm ? still happier far than I !

5.

" I, to whom life refuses all things ! all
Life's joy in earth, air, water !   Still too tall
    The tiniest stem that bears the lowliest flower
For me to climb ! too rough air's lightest sigh
For me to ride ! the nearest dewdrop, dry
    Ere I can reach it !   All, beyond my power !

All, save to disappear—go down—go by—
Sink out of life, not having lived—and die!"

6.

The dying sun the insect's dying moan
O'erheard, and answer'd from his falling throne,
    "Mourn not! I even, I, the sun, go down,
Sink, and drop into darkness. Look at me!"
—He sinks. In pompous purple, pillows he,
    His kingly forehead, girt with golden crown,
And, slowly, with delight his gaze grows dim,
Seeing earth's sadness for the loss of him.

7.

Delicious homage of a dear dismay
Paid to the happy, when they pass away,
    By grief not theirs! Beneath him, prostrate, lies
A world that worships him; and everywhere
Therein he finds some record rich and fair
    Of his own power. He sinks: and wistful eyes
His pathway follow to its glorious bourn.
He sinks: and longing voices sigh " Return !"

8.

He passes: but he hath not pass'd in vain.
He passes, proving by life's loss its gain,
    And bearing with him what he leaves behind.
He goes: rejoicing. " All that I have given

Memory makes mine again, and makes it even
  Mine more completely than before. I shined
Rising and setting. All my light was shown,
And all my force was felt." Thus suns go down.

9.

The boastful orb's last glories, lingering,
That cripple smote. " Go, glories ! tell your king,"
  Smiling he said, "go, him that sent you tell,
Not all so wretched as I deem'd was I.
Since I have seen how suns go down, thereby
  School'd have I been to know, and value well,
What they, the happy,—they that have it not,—
Would fain filch even from a wretch's lot,

10.

" The grandeur of its utter desolation."
All glowing with rebuke and shamed vexation
  The braggart sun's resentful blushes burst,
As o'er the deep, whose surface, and no more,
His glory gilt, he, slowly sinking, bore
  This knowledge gain'd : that Misery at her worst
Hath one poor grace of tragic interest
Proud Pleasure vainly envies at his best.

XXXVI.

FORGIVE AND FORGET.

1.

" Forgive ! forget ! In haste I spoke.
My speech was rash. Resent it not.
Their words unwill'd my lips revoke.
Stretch out thy hand. Be all forgot."
But stunn'd, and still'd, the listener stood.
From stricken heart to sullen brain
Rebounding beat the insurgent blood,
Then clogg'd the gates of life again.

2.

Those rosy roads where tranquil Thought
And Feeling once, like merchant peers,
Embracing mix'd the treasures brought
From their harmonious hemispheres ;
In these, Resentment, outraged Pride,
Wrong'd Honour, Wrath, and rebel Doubt
Now strove, with forces wandering wide,
From Reason's stately ranks thrown out.

3.

" ' Forgive ?   Forget ?'   'Tis lightly said,"
    The sullen answer came at last
Half-crusht, as thro' the spikes it sped
    Of Pride's portcullis—teeth shut fast.
" ' Forgive ! forget !'   And in my place,
    Say what wouldst thou, the wronger, do ? "
" I swear it, as I hope for grace,
    I would forgive, forgetting too !

4.

" And oh that in thy place I were,
    The wronger thou, and mine the wrong !
Nay, hold me to the oath I swear,
    And try me if it hold not strong."
" Man, words are hasty : even so
    Thyself hast said."—" Not hasty this !
O trust it ! try it ! ask or do
    Whate'er thou wilt."—" *Thou* will'st it ?"—" Yes."

5.

A blow . . .   and he that spake the last
    Beneath the bank where they two stood
Was rolling wrapt in foam, and fast
    Borne onward by the boisterous flood.
He beats the blinding wave with strength :
    Chill'd, shaking, aching, drench'd, to shore

He struggles : climbs the bank at length :
    And feebly feels alive once more.

                        6.

" Forgive ! forget !   I struck in haste.
    My blow was rash.   Resent it not.
Is wrong forgiven not wrong effaced ?
    Stretch out thy hand.   Be all forgot."
In wrathful mood he turn'd about,
    Remember'd—realised—forgave—
And, with a rueful smile, held out
    His right hand dripping from the wave.

                        7.

" Nay, overhasty still !   First dry
    You chilly drench that drips amain,
For who would care to embrace (not I !)
    A slobber'd gutter retching rain ? "
" Unjust ! " he cried.   " Take witness, heaven,
    Struck, sicken'd, soak'd to a sop by thee,
The shock, the shame, I have forgiven,
    Nor mine the fault if chill'd I be.

                        8.

" My garments drip, my blood runs cold,
    My limbs are loosed, my lips are blue,
And if I live till I grow old,
    'Twill be, methinks, no thanks to you.

I heed not how my hurts were got,
    I only know they hurt me yet;
But all, it seems, suffices not,
    Half-drown'd, you'd have me still *not wet!*"

9.

" 'Tis well! Thou understand'st me now.
    I, too, can strive : I, too, can brave
What Friendship feels from Friendship's blow :
    Can pluck my soul from out the wave
Of overwhelming wrath and shame,
    Reach shore, and, shivering there (like thee)
Embrace my friend. But not the same
    As Friendship was can Friendship be.

10.

" For lost to love, tho' love may last,
    Is all that love must needs forgive ;
And, tho' forgot, the painful past
    Its prey forgets not. Maim'd we live.
In memory's haunts a horror grows,
    That marks one unremember'd spot ;
And still the hoary hemlock blows
    Where blows the blue forget-me-not."

XXXVII.

THE MOUNTAINS OF TIME.

THE rest that man runs after lures the wretch
From every place where he at rest may be ;
So that his legs are ever on the stretch,
And not one moment of repose hath he.
This frenzy is in certain folks so strong
That, when they find the pavement of the city
Where they walk up and down the whole day long
Not rough enough, however hard and gritty,
It is their wont, some once or twice a year,
To slip away, as wild as hawk or merlin,
From all that city folks hold justly dear
In London, Paris, Rome, Vienna, Berlin,
And seek out mountain places nature made
On purpose for uncomfortable walking.
To swell the number of these fools, I paid
A visit to the Alps ; which, after stalking
Thro' stony vales, I reach'd, and sought repose
Fatiguingly a whole flea-bitten night,
Outfidgeted in a chill Châlet, close
By a green Glacier.   There, before tho' light

I from bed's antisoporific rose,
And set forth booted on my bootless road;
Wondering which first would wear the other out,
The mountain or the boots that o'er it strode.
But both the granite strong and leather stout
Remain'd intact : and tho' to own it loth,
'Tis I that was worn out between them both.
And, when I reach'd the summit where I thought
To pluck pure rapture, life's high alpine flower,
Faint in the snow I stumbled, and besought
My guide to let me sleep away the hour
'Twas settled we must pass there.   He replied
" As *Monsieur* pleases : but make haste he must."
" I'll sleep, then, in a hurry, friend," I sigh'd.
The good man nodded : fish'd a cheese and crust
Out of his wallet ; sat down at my side ;
And munch'd his breakfast while his watch he kept.
Dim round about me wink'd the prospect wide,
Down sank my heavy eyelids, and I slept.

Or slept not ? That's the question. Sleep or waking,
No change of scene across my vision came.
The mountains, which I had erewhile been taking
Such stupid pains to mount, with frozen frame
Still clasp'd the picture which, of Fancy's making
Or Nature's own, was round me, still the same.
The only change (for which I can't account)
Was that my sense of lassitude was gone,
And force was mine to pass from mount to mount,
For miles and miles, still upward and still on.

But what is certainly just now surprising
Is that I felt not then the least surprise
Either at this continual uprising
And journeying onward, just as the bird flies,
Or at the strange means of mine own devising
I found within me (how, I can't surmise)
Of getting, to my mute interrogation,
From all those mountains, marvellous replies.

Much this discovery pleased me as a new one.
And to a modest mamelary peak
Which, tho' an Alp (a genuine and a true one)
Yet, being milder-minded, so to speak,
Of aspect than the rest (who seem'd to view one
With countenances anything but meek)
Inspired me with less awe than all his brothers,
I said as much. " Ay," musingly quoth he,
" The others speak not."—" Friend," said I, " what
        others ?"
" The other mountains," short he answer'd me.
" What other mountains ?" With a touch of mirth
Sublime, he laugh'd " The mountains of the earth."
" Pray, may I ask, then, of what kind they be,
The mountains I've the honour of addressing ?"
" Certainly. Mountains, not of Space, are we,"
He answer'd, " but of Time."—" Of Time ?" confessing
Imprudently mine ignorance, said I,
" This is the first time I have ever heard
That Time has mountains. Pray what are they made of ?"
As tho' he thought this question most absurd,

Mine Alp survey'd me sternly, icily ;
Then with a slight shrug I felt sore afraid of
Half loosed an avalanche, and grumbled " Pooh, man !
Are they not peers and kinsmen, Time and Space ?
And pray to Time, the peer of Space, do you, man,
Deny his rights, his mountains ?"—" Heaven forbid,
   no ! "
I hasten'd to reply. " But, save Your Highness,
I know not (heartily I wish I did know !)
Nor can I " (here I stammer'd, seized with shyness)
" Imagine what they're made of. As for Space,
Why, all the earth affords to Space material
For mountain-making. But that's not the case
With Time, which is " . . . " What's Time ?" mock-
   magisterial
Of mien, he interposed in accents quizzical,
" What's Time ? "
         Now, tho' 'tis true I might have quoted
A dozen learnèd authors metaphysical
Who have . . . well, well, not wasted, but devoted
A deal of time to the consideration
Of what Time is,—yet (as with shame I noted)
Ere I had time to bring out one quotation,
Contemptuously looking down on me,
My questioner relieved the hesitation
His question caused me ; for " Whate'er Time be,"
He added, answering his own query, " Time,
Whose child am I . . . . Tho', if I say I *am*,
Since naked truth's too freezingly sublime
I use, for your sake, a mere verbal sham :

For, truth to say, I'm nothing of the kind,
And Time is nothing, and there's nothing true.
But that's beyond the limits of your mind,
And naturally bounded point of view.
Oh, no offence, man ! Certes you'd not find
Such terms offensive, if you only knew
The advantage of those bounds ; wherein confined,
Man's reason moves with accuracy thro'
The crowded thoroughfares of sense, that wind
In all directions up and down his brain.
These bounds are paved off pathways which allow
The poor foot-passenger, who else were slain,
Keeping along the narrow tracks they show,
To walk securely, and escape the train
Of steeds and chariots that, fast speeding, flow
And flash all round him, in a roaring tide
Certain to crush him if he once broke thro'
His pavement barriers upon either side.
So, to the point. We here, who people Time,
As bodies people Space,—the Hours are we.
The Past upheaves us. Some of us, sublime,
And others lowly, as no doubt you see.
That's as Time makes us, of what men make *him*.
I'm but the Hour of a small office clerk,
Whose whole life was so quiet, dim, and prim,
There's nothing in me to invite remark.
The man who made what Time hath made of me
Lived seventy years ; full fifty years of which
He served the State. When just about to be
Promoted to a post that was the pitch

Of his life's aim (tho' naught to boast of) he,
Poor devil, died an hour too soon.   And thus
The mouse with which I am parturient
Remains within me, evermore, a *mus*
Nondum obortus.   His own fault, I grant.
But since your time is short, make much of us.
Seize the occasion.   Ask whate'er you want.
Many a point remains yet to discuss.
Question the higher Hours."

      I took the hint;
And, having scarcely time to question Time,
Address'd a mount whose purple brows did print
The azure air with pines, that strove to climb
From cloud to cloud into the golden tint
That wrapp'd his summit from the rosy prime.
And "I," said he, " am, in a lover's life
The longest Hour.   For ten impatient years
He, with relentless fortune, lived at strife.
At length love triumph'd over foes and fears.
And in a wood, where she had sworn to meet him,
The coming of his mistress did he wait,
While every rustling leaf conspired to cheat him,
Mocking her steps.   She came—an hour too late.
And, in that hour, such doubts and such despairs
Convulsed his amorous imagination
That I became volcanic unawares,
And choking with internal conflagration,
As you perceive."

     But I, the truth to say,
Perceived not even the slightest indication

Of fires internal in that mountain grey.
Tho', after somewhat closer contemplation,
I spied, 'tis true, a bare patch on his pate,
Which some long empty crater might have been ;
But I believe 'twas only baldness.
                       Straight
I turn'd me towards a giant glacier, green
With hideous glooms.   "What art thou?" I ex-
    claim'd.
" I," sigh'd the icy Horror, and his breath
Froze the blood in me when his name he named,
" Am the Last Hour of one condemn'd to death
For having murder'd life.   Look at me close.
Throughout the Hour I am, one after one,
All the lost moments of that man's life rose
Up to the surface of his soul.   Deeds done,
Days undone, wild desires, and wicked wishes,
Pure joys defiled, and faded memories fond.
One after one they rose up like dead fishes
To the sick surface of a poison'd pond.
He, in this Hour a hundred times eternal,
A child once more, the games of childhood play'd ;
Felt on his brow the kiss of lips maternal ;
A father's counsels heard and disobey'd ;
Far, far away, by flowery paths infernal,
From innocence, repose, and virtue stray'd ;
Felt in his breast love's primal passion burning,
The pang of jealousy's envenom'd dart,
The shock of faith betray'd, the bitter turning
Of love to hate, the ravage of the heart,

Despair, debauchery, destruction, crime,
Conscience, and memory—the soul's last cry!
Behold me. All the emptiness of Time,
And all the wretchedness of Life, am I!"

Smitten with fear, I fled. Nor dared I deem
My soul in safety till I 'scaped the sight
Of that atrocious solitude. My dream
Meanwhile pursued me till I reach'd a height
Surpassing all the others. 'Twas so high
That I perceived below me, far below,
The tallest Alps no bigger to mine eye
Than grains of salt. Naught breathed between the
        brow
Of this stupendous berg and the bare sky.
Oh never yet with such a load of snow
Was earth encumber'd! "Here, at last," said I,
"Must be the Chimborazo, nothing less,
Of human thought. For surely, surely, he
Who raised to such a height the heaviness
Of this all-else-surpassing pile must be
Earth's master-mind. Time meets eternity,
Stretch'd to this altitude." Then loud I cried
"O Atlas, Atlas! tell me, who created
Thy giant form?" Long while no voice replied,
And in the silence of the waste I waited
Wondering, what bard had built this mighty epos:
At length, a plaintive, sleepy whisper sigh'd
"I am the weariest Hour yet known to fate,
Pass'd by a schoolboy, in midsummer tide,

Condemn'd, for misdemeanours, to translate
A dozen chapters of Cornelius Nepos."

Soon as that voice I heard, I seem'd to see
And feel myself transform'd—evaporated,
Then again frozen—and, at last, to be
That mountain in wide azure isolated.
Or, rather, seem'd that mountain part of me.
For I remember'd that my life had dated
Just such an hour.   My soul became one yawn.
My lassitude return'd.   Again I stumbled
And sank down, just where I had sunk at dawn,
As faintly " *Alcibiades*," I mumbled,
" *Cliniæ filius, Atheniensis*" . . .

" Come, wake, sir !   Time's up, and we've miles to
        make yet."
My guide's voice thus recall'd me to my senses.
I rose, and rubb'd mine eyes ; and, scarce awake yet,
Look'd round—and recognised them every one :
The amorous and agèd Don-Juanic
Volcano, with his bald head in the sun,
Proud of his long-quench'd spritely spurts volcanic ;
The mamelon in labour with its mouse ;
The convict's frozen conscience ; that titanic
Alp-upon-alp of taskwork tyrannous ;
At whose sight, I sprang forward with a thrill
Of anguish, trying vainly to complete
My chapter of Cornelius Nepos still.
The guide, in front, cried " Eh sir, mind your feet !

Nor look down yonder till we've turn'd the hill.
The tug's to come yet." In his winding-sheet
The convict glared upon me, grim and chill.
" How call you yonder glacier, my good man, eh ?"
" Sir," said the guide, " we call it Le Condamné.
Mind where you step now."—" Yes," I murmur'd,
    " yes,
Atheniensis Alcibiades " . . .

XXXVIII.

CONSERVATION OF FORCE.

I.

A MUSICIAN once, in the twilight time,
Musing sat by the instrument
Whose keys knew how, with a kindred chime,
To interpret to him what his musings meant.
Then a picture, the man had seen that day
And, because of its colour or composition,
Had, deep in the soul of him, borne away,
Unmiss'd, from its place in the Exhibition,
Began to suffer a mystic change,
And pass from the soul where its own lay pent
On the wings of a melody wild and strange ;
Which, as 'twere in a dream, his fingers went
Wandering after, over the keys ;
Whose notes were thus scatter'd, and then again blent
Till the twilight was fill'd with the music of these.

2.

But when, like a wind from a land unknown,
That comes and goes with a will of its own,
The strain died out, and left, as it died,
The throbbing silence unsatisfied,
A friend of the player's who, listening, sat
In that twilight chamber beside him, cried
With a sigh, " Continue !"   " Continue what ?
I have not been playing," the player replied,
" But only thinking—ah, thinking ? nay,
But rather dreaming all thought away
About a picture I saw to-day."
" Strange !" said the other ; " and whilst unto thee
I was listening, just ere thy music fainted,
A poem impress'd itself on me,
As clear as a picture freshly painted.
Farewell, ere I lose it !"   Then home went he,
And wrote the poem to which that strain
Had changed itself in the poet's brain.

3.

This poem another painter read ;
And it haunted that other painter's head,
Till of it another picture he made ;
Which, like the first, was exhibited.

4.

When, after many a year was past,
Those pictures twain were uphung at last
Side by side on the self-same wall
Of the same museum, they did not fall
Into the arms of each other, the one
Crying " My father !" the other " My son !"
Tho' in line direct was their filiation.
But, like two athletes, they struggled and fought
Against each other without cessation.
And men, taking part in the contest, brought
Daily, to deepen it, fresh contestation.
Critic and craftsman, with praise or blame,
Choosing their side in the battle, became,
These the passionate partisans
Of the style of the earlier master ; those
Of the style of the later ; until two clans
Of disciples, two schools of art, arose,
Which, in turn, put forth for the world's applause
Masterpieces of different kinds ;
The unlike effects of a single cause,
One force transmitted thro' many minds.

5.

For, tho' none of the critics of this was aware,
And not even the craftsmen the secret knew,
Yet all these pictures the offspring were
Of a single picture—the first of the two.

XXXIX.

HOMERIDES.

1.

Nature hath given the Stag a wondrous gift.
Love, and the force that loving hearts doth lift
To lofty courage by the sweet desire
Of winning love, have with creative fire
Gone to his burning brain, and thence burst out
In that brave crest he proudly bears about.
Thus, in love's complete beauty arm'd, he roams
The gusty realms of passion, and becomes
A living tempest; with whate'er in storm
Hath being—motion swift, majestic form,
Strife, rapture, peril, and the pomp of power.
Then, like the storm which hath its one wild hour
And passes, he—his passion once subdued
By surfeit fierce—returns to solitude.

2.

A Beetle, burrowing where a Stag had been,
Humm'd " Ha, brave buck! here hast thou left, I ween,

To me who live upon thy leavings, fine
And fit material for a crown like thine !
For I surmise, since matter's everywhere,
That everything is matter.   Maidens, fair
And pure, I've seen, who stoop'd to pluck and place
(Charm'd by the beauty of it and the grace)
In that sweet haunt of the Hesperides,
The guardian of whose hidden apples is
Jealous Desire, some flow'ret haply fed
On the foul scrapings of the cattle-shed :
And, if such filth could into beauty bud,
Beauty, thou art but metamorphosed mud !
Eureka !   Here must the Stag's secret lie.
Could I but catch it, doubtless also I
Should get the grace to which my soul aspires,
And sprout those horns the horn-mad world admires."

3.

With which intent, on what he found he fed ;
Till gradually from his insect head
The superfluity of matter there
Oozed out in frontal ornaments that were
Not all unlike the antlers of a stag.
Then, quite contented, he began to brag,
" A stag am I, and brave mine antlers be ! "

4.

And yet he was but a stag-beetle, he.

MORAL.

The poet's form is to his followers known.
The poet's secret is the poet's own.
'Tis born and buried in the poet's soul :
Passion its prelude, solitude its goal.

XL.

POINTS DE VUE—POINT DE VUE.

1.

A DWELLER in a city of the plain,
  Bound on a journey to a mountain land,
First pray'd a famous traveller to explain
  How best he might behold, and understand,
The rumour'd wonders of that lofty region,
For by report the name of them was legion.

2.

"There's but one way," the traveller replied,
  "Beneath the highest mountain of them all
There lies a little town. Get there a guide :
  Then, rest not till you reach its summit tall.
The ascent is difficult. I grant 'tis double—
But it is also twice well worth—the trouble.

3.

" For by this means not only will you be
  Rewarded with an admirable view,

But 'tis, indeed, the *only* means to see
  At one wide eyesweep, adequately true
And comprehensive in its contemplation,
The whole of that high land's configuration."

4.

Struck by the justice of his friend's advice,
  Which promised an incomparable sight,
And full of ardour, on his enterprise
  The man set forth.   He reach'd the inn at night
Commended by the traveller; went to bed,
Slept well, waked early, rose, dress'd, breakfasted;

5.

And from the casement of his room could see
  That mighty mountain clad in cloud and snow.
The guide inform'd him that, to mount it, three
  Good days 'twould take him; to descend it, two.
But he before him had a fortnight's time,
Nor need begin in haste that task sublime.

6.

So he resolved to make a first essay
  By visiting the hills and slopes that lower,
Lapping the flanks of that high mountain, lay
  Like housetops huddled round a minster tower;
This promenade was picturesque, and soon
Completed in one pleasant afternoon.

7.

'Tis true the prospects it unfolded each
    One corner only of the picture show'd :
But all the others he proposed to reach,
    One after one, by the same easy road,
Encouragingly smooth for a beginner,
The following days 'twixt breakfast-time and dinner.

8.

" For thus shall I have witness'd all," he said,
    " In course of time ; and witness'd all without
Foregoing for that purpose board or bed,
    And being thoroughly fatigued no doubt."
So said, so done ; and home again content,
Having climb'd all those little hills, he went.

9.

Their various points of view had pleased him well ;
    Their slopes were wooded, and their tops were
        green :
From each he saw across the neighbouring dell :
    But saw no further : for each crest had been
In turn commanded by some other crest,
Just high enough to overtop the rest.

10.

In silence did his travell'd friend receive
    The tale of those short journeys ; and replied

" The charm of your excursion, I perceive,
    Lay in those little slopes that, every side,
Shut out the distance ; hills climb'd yesterday
Bounding to-morrow's prospect all the way.

11.

" With not more trouble, and in shorter time,
    You, following my counsel, would have seen
The whole horizon's airy orb sublime
    Reveal'd beyond each decorated screen
Of those low mountains. For that summit tall
Of which I told you doth surmount them all.

12.

" I, in man's thought, as 'twere a bird behold,
    Born to disport itself in space, with wing
Unfetter'd by the wires, tho' they be gold,
    Of any cage. Albeit I grant birds sing
In cages. But that, doubtless, is a merit
They from the freeborn songsters do inherit.

13.

" And better, to my thinking, one high note
    Dropt by the soaring skylark from the sky
Than all that's warbled from a cageling's throat.
    Minds are there, too, whose natural home is high ;
One word they drop in passing is worth more
Than tutor'd twitterers twitter by the score."

XLI.

PYRRHONISM,

OR,

THE HAUNTED HEN.

1.

A HEN, whom the bounty of Providence made
A parent prolific, with motherly pride
Every day a fresh egg in the henroost laid,
Which to hatch into life she then patiently tried.
But, whilst on those eggs she was brooding warm
In a placid glow of parental pleasure,
Chill was the change as she spied with alarm
A Weasel, who watch'd her, aware of her treasure.
And this Hen henceforth was so haunted by
The chilly charm of that Weasel's eye,
That, night by night, in her dreaming sleep
It was ever the self-same dream she dream'd ;
How, changed to a Weasel, she crept in the deep
Of the dark to the henroost ; and, stealthily seem'd
With the craft of a Weasel to suck and destroy
Those eggs that, by day, were the poor fowl's joy.

2.

This double identity, made up of two—
Her waking and sleeping self—at last
The Hen's life into confusion threw,
And over it, daily and nightly, cast
The spell of a twofold trouble.   By day
She lived in such dread of her midnight dream
That at length not an egg was she able to lay:
Yet this daily sterility did not redeem
From its nightly plague her spirit tormented,
When she, by the dream's transforming power,
Changed into a Weasel, was discontented
At finding no more any eggs to devour.

3.

" Ah, had I," she sigh'd, " but the gift to forget,
I might hope to recapture lost happiness yet !
Then, by day, with a spirit unvext should I
Taste the soothing sweets of maternity,
Whilst the ravisher's raptures of cruel delight
Would be mine, with young victims to ruin, by night.
But alas ! as it is, I can neither enjoy
The rude libertine's lust, nor the love of the mother ;
Who, combining two selves that each other destroy,
Fail to realise either the one or the other ! "

MORAL.

So are we : who, both author and critic in one,
Miss the comfort accorded to either alone.
By alternate creative and critical powers
Is our suffering identity sunder'd and torn :
And the tooth of the critic that's in us devours
Half the author's conceptions before they are born.

XLII.

THE MOUNTAIN AND THE MARSH.

A REVERIE.

1.

Low natures cannot even forgive the good
    Another's greatness on their fate entails.
'Twixt sea and land a granite Mountain stood,
    No further than a wounded bittern trails
His broken wing, beyond a Swampy Flood
    Foul with green ooze. The inland-blowing gales
That died upon his summit did bequeath
A quiet climate to the land beneath.

2.

The gracious image of this Mountain slept
    Unruffled in the dark of that dull Meer;
Where rarely even a lazy ripple crept
    To bid the bulrush shake his languid spear

O'er livid streaks of stagnant scum, that kept
    The calm contour, with every outline clear,
And all the colours of the portraiture,
    Tho' painted on a filthy surface, pure.

3.

But daily ever, when the sun was low,
    And, in a rosy reflex aureole,
The guardian Mount's grey head began to glow,
    From out his marble-breasted body stole,
And sidled, lingering to the lowland slow,
    What seem'd the Mountain's disembodied soul :
A stealthy, shy, and solitary elf,
The insubstantial semblance of himself.

4.

Over the fens it fared, where dreamy rows
    Of cattle farmward moved their wandering camp ;
But scarce had reach'd the rivage, ere there rose
    Resentful challenge from that churlish Swamp ;
Hoarse as the choral croak that overflows
    In gleaming eves of Spring the shallows damp,
And reedy brinks, of their spawn-mantled bogs,
From many thousand throats of querulous frogs :

        " Halt, vagabond ! halt where thou art !
        Nor insult with thy presence abhorr'd
        The floor of my palace.   Depart,
        Silly slave of an insolent lord !

"And thou, broad braggart, I pray
 Invade not my virginal bed.
Let the earth to thy foot give way,
 And the heaven to thy horrible head :

"Parade thine imperial mantle,
 Which this lackey behind thee doth bear,
Till it leaves not uncover'd a cantle
 Of the subject world—elsewhere :

"But sully not with it my fountain !
 Queen am I in my realm : and thine,
Tho' it prison the sun, proud mountain,
 I allow not alliance with mine."

5.

The gracious Mount, aware of his wrong'd worth,
 Made generous answer in grave tones and sweet ;
Around him gazing, east, west, south, and north,
 With kingly calm that claim'd attention meet ;
While that sick shrew spat her foul spittle forth
 And in her own filth wallow'd at his feet.
His voice was as the sighing of a breeze
Born on the bosom of the boundless seas :

"Friend, leave to the human race
 The inhuman habit of war !
To each in the world his place,
 And we are whatever we are.
To each his good and his ill :
 And the ill of the good made mine
Is that, doom'd to forever be still,
 I must ever for motion pine.
The bees and the butterflies
 Hover over the blossom bells ;
And the birds in the balmy skies,

And the feathery-sail'd seed-cells,
They wander about ; and I,
As I watch them, wish that I were
A bee, or a butterfly,
Or a little bird of the air !
But to each in the world his place,
And to every ill some good.
Unto me my granite base,
And to thee thy shelter'd flood.
Yet O, how the spirit in me
Is troubled when bound, alas,
To this granite base, I see
(As the pure winds over me pass)
The leaflet leap on the tree,
And the flow'ret nod in the grass,
And the long grass wave on the lea,
And the reed in the wan morass !
And thou, too ?   Dost thou not feel
(When the sedge to the low wind sighs)
Sweet tremors over thee steal,
And a rapture of ripples arise ?
Say, wouldst thou not follow the wind
In a wave of wonder away,
Were thy waters unconfined
By their osier cradle grey ?
The hungry ocean, hidden
By me from the heedless land ;
Which it leaps to devour, and, chidden,
Falls back at my mute command :
Fares it better than thou who, rockt
By low-breathing winds, and fann'd
To sleep, liest safely lockt
In the hollow of earth's huge hand ?
No ! it suffers the same effect,
Only all on a vaster scale.
And if thy small fleets unwreckt
Are but blown by a baby gale,
(Dead leaflets gaily speckt,
With a spider's web for a sail)
Whilst yonder (a floating fort)
The battle-ship huge, that mocks

The enemy's bellowing port,
Sinks shatter'd on surfy rocks.
Who shelters thee, thankless Queen,
Secure in thy small domain ?
I, the friend of whose shade serene
Thy churlish lips complain !
I, the giant who stand between
Thy rest and the roaring main ! "

6.

The brave old Mount, by wounding weathers scarr'd,
    O'er the low-sunken, safely-shelter'd lea,
Which his grey head from howling gusts did guard,
    And o'er the rolling ridges of the sea,
Sent far his grave, calm, satisfied regard ;
    Then glanced athwart that gloomy Swamp, but she
Sigh'd only, sullen, from her sedgy beach,
As, smiling, he resumed, in mountain-speech :

    " O rapturous, wandering wings,
      O rivulets, running for ever,
      O winds, clouds, waves, happy things !
    I, that never may follow you, never
    Taste with you a traveller's bliss,
      As ye roam over moorland and meadow,
    I, at least (and who grudges me this ?)
    Send forth on his travels my Shadow.
    'Tis a gentle and timorous sprite,
    That never, except when night
    Is falling, ventures far ;
    And, albeit inquisitive, most
    Discreet ; not given to boast,
    As other travellers are ;
    Pure, tho' it sleep in the slime ;
    Shy as a young bird thrown
    Unfledged from its nest sublime ;
    Yet with secret joys of its own ;

And by only two at a time
Is its intimate sweetness known.
But of any two lovers, I pray,
Be it ask'd if they love not the shade :
And the happy ones, boy and maid,
Will blush as they turn away
Sighing and smiling, afraid
Its secret bliss to betray ;
Whilst the others, whose hearts be cleft
For the grave of a lost love, laid
Dead in its birthplace,—'reft
Of the hopes that with shadows have play'd,
Will sigh ' Our sole happiness left
Is to wander and weep in the shade.'
Why is it ?   They know not why.
'Tis an antique mystery.
This nursling of Night's lone heart
Hath known sorrow, and learn'd to be still
But it cherisheth, pure and apart,
In its own chaste silence chill,
A memory, mighty, immense
Of passionate love and pain ;
A memory mixt with a sense
Of deep desire and disdain ;
A memory made intense
By a love that was loved in vain !"

7.

Here, soughing in the sedge, the Water made
    A restless moan of weary resignation ;
As who should say ' I heed not what is said,
    Altho' I hear it.'   And a dull pulsation
Darken'd the melancholy moonbeam laid
    To listless rest along the late stagnation
Of the now rippled liquid in her lone
Low reedy creeks.   The musing Mount went on :

" Ere Love was acquainted with Sorrow,
   Ere Eve was a wife or a mother,
Ere the even was 'ware of the morrow,
   Or yet either had banisht the other,
   In Eden the Night and the Morn
   Were dissever'd as soon as born.
The *Fiat Lux* thunders thro' heaven !
And, awakening Creation, hath riven
   The resonant portals of Light.
All gushing with glorious surprises
The Sun, in his royalty, rises,
   And bursts on the realm of the Night.
He comes ! and the Silence profound,
That hath watch'd with droopt wings spread afar
Over Night's maiden dreams, at the sound
Of the steps of the conquering star,
   Is smitten and scatter'd in flight.
And he comes : lifts the veil from her breast,
   And sees naked the beautiful Night.
Venit, vidit . . . . who knows not the rest ?
   O what an awakening was there !
What rapture ! and O what despair !
   One moment hath ruin'd forever
Love and power.   Alas, he, and she?
Light and Darkness ?   Impossible ! Never,
   O never, such union can be !
Such, of old, was the destiny vain
   Of that incompatible twain :
And such is the endless condition
   Of Passion, the child of disdain
And desire,—life and death in transition !
Hope snatcht from the breast of despair
Is hers, and a life that is death ;
For she breathes in the deadliest air,
   And she dies of but one quiet breath.
Her food is the fruit that's forbidden :
   Her pleasure a prayer never granted :
Her strength is a wish that is chidden :
   And her weakness the thing that she wanted !"

8.

High winds, that vex'd not the still earth, began
   To smite the upmost heaven. With fitful light
The stricken moon thro' fleecy cloudlets ran.
   The Mountain, from that drift of dark and bright
Which o'er him glimpsed in alternation wan,
   Caught mystic motion ; and, in spectral flight
Hovering above the melancholy plain,
The spirit that was in him spake again :

    " And the Sun, never-resting, forsaken,
      And fierce in his anguish of light,
      Cries thro' heaven ' Where art thou ? awaken,
      And return to me, fugitive Night ! '
      But she, whose unsatisfied lover
      Thus renews his importunate flame,
      Where hides she ? with what does she cover
      Her beauty, her babe, and her shame ?
      Ask yon quivering splendours, that swim
      The blue dark in bright shoals overspread,
      If they know in what solitude dim
      Night is hiding her desolate head :
      And those liveried lackeys of Light
      (In the cause of Light's glory enlisted)
      Will answer ' What is it, the Night ?
      'Tis a myth that has never existed ! '
      Ask the planet whose golden urn
      Flows over with flaming amber
      As he, courtier-like, taketh his turn
      In the sun's bright antechamber :
      He laugheth ' The Sun is my king :
      The fallen are soon forgot :
      I follow the conquering :
      And the Night ? . . . I know her not.'
      And the sliding meteor will say,
      As he falls in a fiery drop,

'Who cares? I have miss'd my way,
And can neither retrace it nor stop.'
And, blushing, the Dawn will sigh
' I awaked ere my dreams were done.
They were fair ; but I know not, I,
If I dream'd of the Night . . . or the Sun ?'
And, if all things else deny her,
Renounce the Night or ignore,
Go, ask of the ghostly fire
That hovers on that pale shore,
Where, embark'd in its phantom comet,
The wandering embryon waits
God's finger to fashion from it
A world of yet unknown fates :
It will mutter ' I mark'd her creeping,
By the light of a latent moon,
Between two worlds and weeping,
Like a beggar that asks a boon
At the gates of a rich man's place,
With a shamed and sorrowful mien :
And I think it was to embrace
Her sleeping babe unseen.'

" That babe, is it Bliss?　But aloud
Breathe the name of it never !　At best
'Tis a treasure that, risk'd if avow'd,
Is in fear and in peril possest :
Whose possessor, as one that encroacheth
Upon ground that's forbidden, by night,
All atremble his treasure approacheth
But to bury it deep out of sight.
And, O thou to whom never before
Hath been utter'd this antique story,
Insult not the shade (tho' no more
Than a shadow it be) of lost glory.
For what it must be at the last
The Present doth ill to scorn.
And the Present shall be the Past
Ere the Future it boasts be born."

9.

Never before that venerable Mount
 Had spoken at such length : nor ever met
A listener in whose ear he could recount
 Without ungracious interruption, yet,
The fancies vague that, like a vented fount
 Whose struggling waters sudden outlet get,
Upwell'd within him, and pour'd wide and free
His secret thoughts in wandering reverie.

10.

But ah ! the old story-teller's pride received
 A sharp rebuff—not loud, but, certes, deep !
When, pausing for an answer, he perceived
 The Water had been all this while asleep.
Sleep thou, too, good old Mount ! with heart ungrieved,
 Tho' heedless ears thy long discourse hold cheap.
Sleep, and good dreams be thine ! There are sins worse
Than too much talk in unregarded verse.

11.

And, if men miss the moral of thy strain,
 Tell them 'tis in themselves, and tell them why.
Wherever croaking commonwealths complain
 Of their old mountain bulwarks and deny
Even the shadow of greatness, where in vain
 Is heard the voice of hoar Authority,
There, lost among the morals of the time,
May haply lurk the moral of thy rhyme.

XLIII.

TELEOLOGY.

1.

THE casement of a chamber in an inn
O'erlook'd a courtyard full of weeds and stones.
And on the stones and weeds that deck'd therein
A haunt of blue-flies, heap'd with offal, bones,
Ordures, and broken pots, and rusty tin,
(Which 'neath this casement made a goodly show)
Out of the lattice from the room within,
A traveller whom it lodged was wont to throw
The soap-suds daily scraped from cheek and chin,
His razor's refuse, mixt with frothy flow
Of basin-rinsings warm ; nor cared a pin
Whose pate might catch such casual chrism.   Below
Upon a dunghill, thirsty, parcht, and thin,
A miserable nettle chanced to grow.

2.

This wretched weed, which else had died of drought,
In the chance rescue of that daily rain

Its own advantage found ; and, free from doubt,
Perceiving in it adaptation plain
Of means to a beneficent design,
Exclaim'd " O Urticarian Jupiter,
What wisdom is there in thy will divine !
Who dost on all thy universe confer
Convincing proofs of providence benign.
By what supreme administrative feat
Hast thou contrived for me, thy grateful child,
Recurrence of this tepid torrent sweet !
Which every morning with its moisture mild
Revives my strength, and heals all hurtful heat.
Whilst, regularly rising day by day,
Thy gracious sun rules all the rolling year,
Warms the wide world with his benignant ray,
And in their season bids my buds appear.
How admirably organised is all
This wondrous world ! whose aspect everywhere
Reveals to reverent thought, in great and small,
Contrivance order'd with consummate care
Its maker's purpose to fulfil : which is
THE HAPPINESS OF NETTLES.   Mighty Jove,
On me thy mercies have not fallen amiss.
Thy purpose I divine : and, proud to prove
My part therein, each seed of mine that settles
Shall do its best to fill the world with nettles."

3.

Thus, in good faith, the thriving weed adored
The patronage of providence ; and, wedding,

The graceful action to the grateful word,
Began to cover with a verdant spreading
Of stinging stuff the filth it chanced to find
A root in (how it knew not, neither why)
'Mid shards, and scurf, and scum of every kind ;
Convinced it was promoting worthily
The strenuous effort of almighty Jove
A virgin nettle forest to create.

4.

Meanwhile, the traveller in the room above
Had finish'd the affair for which of late
He had been lingering in that inn.   The man
Was (as the Fabulist forgot to state
When he this Fable in hot haste began)
A manufacturer in search of coal
To feed his forges at the cheapest rate.
And, having visited at last the whole
Coal-bearing region, rummaged it about,
And made his choice, now, wishing to get rid
Of the rejected samples, he threw out
(To join the other refuse that unchid
Sprawl'd in the heat upon that heap of dung)
The residue of his unclean collection.

5.

By woeful luck there chanced to fall among
That grimy clan, in their abrupt ejection,

A heavy lump of carboniferous schist,
Which flat upon the flowering nettle flopp'd ;
Whose crusht philosophy, collapsing, miss'd
Benignant purpose in the blow that stopp'd
Philosophising with a pang of pain.
" Fatality, and malediction !" hiss'd
The mangled weed with indignation vain,
" What Demon rules this universe, and slays
Without a purpose, making earth one hell ?
Blind Chance it is ! and since blind Chance obeys
No guiding law, methinks it might as well
Have fall'n on either side of me, instead
Of tumbling thus precisely on my head ! "

6.

Uttering this blasphemy the nettle died.
But not before his gaze, fast growing dim,
Had contemplated with a mournful pride
The tumulary pile that cover'd him.
For there he mark'd the impress of a plant
Of perisht centuries.   That antique print
Of vegetable forms no more extant
He took for epitaph, admiring in 't
The grandeur of his race in days gone by,
And " *semper virens !* " was his life's last sigh.

MORAL.

Self-Interest, whiles it prospers, aye believes
Its profit the chief aim of Providence.
And even death's sigil on the tomb deceives
Its vanity with plausible pretence
Of pride in nothingness, abasht no whit
To join HIC JACET to HIC INCIPIT.

XLIV.

COGITO ERGO SUM.

I.

" WHATSOEVER the names whereby men call things,
I ponder, compare, and discriminate all things."

Whose speech?　A philosopher's, say you, this?
If so, then your error is great as his.
'Twas a Grocer's Balance that spoke that speech:
His beam was rusty, his brass scales each
Bumpt and bent; yet as proud he hung
Over the cheating counter, slung
From a bar screw'd fast to a greasy shelf,
As if Themis had hung him aloft herself.

For, having weigh'd all things (butter-pats,
Snuff, cloves, coffee, and salted sprats),
And determined their gravity, great or small,
He believed that he understood them all.

2.

" Now, man," he resumed, with himself agreeing,
"Is an incomplete and impulsive being,
Who, judging of things as they seem to be,
Would misjudge them all, were it not for me.
But his *a priori* I soon put straight
By the solid and readjusting weight
Of my *a posteriori* test.
If at first I feel for a while opprest
By the force of the problem thought presents
To my brain-pan loaded with arguments,
Mine impulse anon is to soar above it,
Contemplate, cogitate, calculate, prove it.
For my reason ever inclines in me
My will, which is for that reason free,
To the truth, where I rest and am satisfied,
Between the extremes upon either side.
There the goal is gain'd, and why further go?
Since I know that I think, what I think I must
    know,
And thus perfect, at last, to the point I come
With my formula *cogito ergo sum*."

3.

Those Weights which the Balance was pleased to call
His arguments, being false weights all,
Knew full well, and with secret glee,
Mock'd at the trick of the whole machine,

" For if Justice had only eyes to see,
That rogue the Grocer had long since been
Hang'd by the neck as he ought to be,"
(These False Weights sneer'd with a surly spleen)
" And thou shouldst have served for his gallows tree.
Thou dost think, and so art?   State the truth as it is,
Thou dost fancy thou thinkest, and thinkest thou art.
Be it so!   It costs nothing to think that or this,
And let each have his fancy.   We, too, for our part,
Have a notion 'tis worth not two penn'orth of twine,
What thou art or thou thinkest.   But spare us, we
          pray,
That absurd ergotistical Ergo of thine,
Which to others must sound disobliging if they
Chance to be without thinking.   For instance, to man,
Who would surely not be what he is if he thought,
And is right; for the main thing's to be, if one can,
And to think about being is nutshell and naught.
As for thee, if thou canst, thou canst do nothing better
Than beget little scales, and take care that they be
Each, if possible, just like its precious begetter,
For the world's tongue is scandalous.   So much for
          thee !
For thine Ergo ; not *cogito*, say, *ergo sum*,
But to *cogito* rather subjoin *ergo est*,
And, at least somewhat nearer the truth wilt thou
          come ;
To thy formula standing, but standing confest
Sole creator of that idiotic creation
Whose silly existence exists at the best

In the depths of thine own idiotic sensation.
And then as for thy will; it obeys the behest
Of the motive that's strongest, a slave and a thrall
To the force we all feel and yet none of us know.
For the rickety tile that is ready to fall
From the top of the roof if the wind blows high
And be smasht to bits in the street below,
First smashing the skull of some passer-by,
Hath a will that's as free every whit as thine own,
And the sense not, at least, to talk nonsense about it,
Down it falls when it must, and it lies where 'tis
    thrown,
By an impulse received from a pressure without it.
That pressure's Necessity. What she pronounces
Finds thee, too, like others, obedient enough.
What is coffee? a pound of it weighs sixteen ounces,
And so much, and no more, does a pound weigh of
    snuff.
This alone, at the most, canst thou know after weigh-
    ing it,
And 'tis but the result of thou knowest not what.
If thou sayest it, 'tis that thou canst not help saying it,
And thou never wilt say a thing truer than that."

4.

Now a metal is iron as hard as nails,
Practical, patient, not easily bored:
But ideas it hates, and against them prevails,
As we often have seen, at the point of the sword.

Whilst the Balance uphung 'twixt the earth and the
  sky,
And by nature responsive to every vibration,
Hovers vague in a realm insubstantial and high
Which seems made for the purpose of pure specu-
  lation.
So that when "sixteen ounces of snuff are a pound-
  weight,"
The Weights cried below to the Balance above,
Tho' he knew not, as we do, that this was unsound
  weight,
He replied, with a shrug, " Well, and what does that
  prove?"
Then, convinced that he had by this interrogation
Their materialist insolence sternly put down,
He return'd with a tremor of self-admiration
To the point out of which the discussion had grown.

5.

And so matters went on, until brought to a stop
By a quite unforeseen and unpleasant event:
When one day on the Grocer's iniquitous shop
The Police made an inquisitorial descent;
Which establish'd the fact that each weight was a
  light one,
That the Balance had in it a tendency strong
To incline to the side that was never the right one,
And the Grocer had known of the trick all along.

The Grocer was fined.　The Police took possession
Of the Balance and Weights.　These the Law handed
　　over
To the anvil and hammer, that made an impression
Upon them from which they will never recover.

6.

In one sack of old iron regardlessly shaken
Do FREE WILL and NECESSITY rust evermore.
To a different system the Grocer has taken,
And he cheats more ingeniously now than before.

XLV.

PHILOSOPHY OF THE LITTLE.

Two cousins (they were but of distant degree,
But blood's thicker than water, and each was a Flea)
Met each other by chance.　Did not History tell
(For the goings of Fleas are inscrutable)
Whereabouts it was in their nightly walk
The dark kinsmen, meeting, fell into a talk
In the usual over-emphatic style
Of friends who, when after a long, long while
They meet unawares, in that unwill'd meeting
Evince, by a nervously-cordial greeting,
Keener care for each other's affairs
Than they honestly feel.　For if one of them wears
A threadbare coat, though as warm perhaps
As the weather in June be the breast it wraps,
At the sight of it something shuts somewhere
In the heart, like a door in a draught of air.
Now one of these two was a fine fat Flea :
To the other, a lean one, " Coz," quoth he,
In a tone of compassionate semi-suspicion
" You seem to be terribly out of condition."

"Alas!" said the lean one, "friend, in me,
The ruin'd though innocent victim you see
Of one fatal error beyond recall.
My means of life I invested all
In the skin of an Ape. It was juicy and fat.
I married in haste on the strength of that,
Had a numerous family, daughters, sons,
Nor was Flea ever father of fairer ones.
Now wife and little ones, all are lost!
Ah! had I but counted the care and cost,
Or had I but dream'd of the danger and toil,
When I settled first on that fertile soil!
I confess my fault. I was taken in.
Who could guess that an Ape has so ticklish a skin?
The brute was prurient, and idle too,
With nothing better all day to do
Than scratch, scratch, scratch ; you conceive the
    despair
Of a flea whose whole livelihood hangs by a hair.
But enough of the miseries *I* have gone thro'.
My illustrious friend how much better with *you*,
Has the world, since we parted, been wagging!" "So,
    so!"
Complacently nodded the other. "I know
Nothing much, on the whole, I can grumble about,
Save a plaguy sharp twinge now and then of the gout.
'Tis the fruit of good fare and the life that I lead
Which is pleasant enough." "So it *must* be, indeed!"
The lean Flea said with a hungry sigh.
"But where are you living?" "Luxuriously

With my friend the Lion." "The Lion? alack!"
The starveling stammer'd as he skipp'd back,
"Have, then, his terrible claws and teeth
Their use forgone? How! dwelling beneath
Those dread conditions, hast thou possest
A single moment of ease or rest?"
Scornfully smiled the superior Flea.
"What are his claws or his teeth to me?
Leonine talons may tear wild bulls,
They cannot fidget a flea. Fear dulls,
O foolish cousin, thy feeble wit.
Apes scratch themselves at each itching fit,
And in public pick out their private fleas,
Not resenting disgust if they get but ease.
Thine own insignificance prudently trust.
A lion bears nobly what nobleness must.
Of a friend's experience this maxim learn,
And I'll warrant you, Cousin, 'twill serve your turn :
From a world of foes wouldst thou live exempt ?
Then shelter thyself in the world's contempt.
'Tis a fortune subscribed by all creatures for thee.
Go, trade on it! safe—if thou art but a flea."

XLVI.

MASTER AT HOME.

PART I.

In grateful memory of each gracious reference
  Made to them by the one and thousand stories
Of Queen Scheherazade,—or duteous deference
  To him in whom its immemorial glories
Their realm attain'd,—the Beasts decreed thy name
  Haroun Alraschid, to the bravest, best,
And noblest of their kings—a king whose fame
  His title merited, as mightiest
Of monarchs leonine. Nor e'er hath been
  That ancient realm so fair and flourishing
At any time before or since, I ween,
  As when Haroun the Illustrious was King.

That Royal lion, like his namesake, loved
  To roam, incognito, his realms by night,
And if—at morn, what time it heedless roved,
  Some subject's stumbling footstep chanced to 'light

Upon a heap of bones, or bloody fleece,
    Where, in the dark, the King of Beasts had been,
Or if, upon the barks of drooping trees
    Some Beaver's tooth, calumniously keen,
Had scored a scandalous chronicle,—what then?
    Who is exempt from scandal?   Not the great.
Are not the mighty paths of mighty men
    Strewn with such ugly traces of the fate
Of little ones?   And what's a sheep or two
    Lost in a lion's glory and renown?
To his high name and famous title true,
    Fear'd and revered was the great Lion Haroun.
But was he happy?   Whosoe'er had seen
    The grace, the beauty, and the loveliness
Of the young Lioness, Haroun's fair Queen,
    Could surely doubt not of the monarch's bliss:
Limbs whose luxurious and majestic mould
    Seem'd by some mighty artist's magic hand
Shaped into gliding form from flexile gold;
    And, what most won the heart of all the land,
Oh, such a nameless charm of grace refined,
    In every movement, queenly feminine,
Of the soft tail that, curving, swept behind,
    And scarcely stirr'd a single sandgrain fine
With its light fringe, yet gave to all the rest
    Expression irresistibly enchanting;
A charm by high-born dames alone possest.
    In short, no beauty to the queen was wanting.
All female charms were hers: and she was his:
    But ah! the heart that every joy possesses

Except one joy, if that one joy it miss,
  All joy in all it hath too often misses !
Oft o'er the king's majestic brow would rise
  The wrinkling shadow of a secret care ;
Oft o'er the orbits of his fervid eyes
  The massive muscle swell'd as though it were
Stung by a sudden inward irritation ;
  Whilst restless swishings of the royal tail
Gave momentary tokens of vexation ;
  Which his proud soul allow'd not to prevail,
But, with impatient toss of the large mane,
  Shook scornful off : then, with a yawn immense,
Half of submission, half of deep disdain,
  Mixt with a supercilious somnolence,
The wide jaws gaped, and he, as one resign'd
  To those small troubles which infest the great,
Stretch'd slow his lordly limbs. The Court divined
  The Monarch's mood : anxieties of State !
Oft, at the dead of night the antler'd Hart,
  Couch'd in the grass beside his spotted Doe,
From restless dreams would tremulously start
  And, heedless, strike his ornamented brow
All scared against the elm-tree's neighbouring bark ;
  When from the far-off, deep-porch'd palace, borne
Along the listening silence of the dark,
  Fierce cries of royal wrath and passionate scorn,
And then the roaring fall, and heavy roll
  Of mighty ones with mighty ones contending
Startled the poor stag's palpitating soul ;
  His straddled slender legs beneath him bending.

His spouse, too, hearing what he heard, half rose,
    Scared for a moment by that ominous sound :
But, when her glance fell on the hornèd brows
    Of her good helpmate conjugally crown'd,
She, with a slight toss of her dainty head,
    (Significant of pacified alarm)
Settled again to sleep in her soft bed
    Safe hid among the forest herbage warm.
And when, next morn, the Monarch sat in Hall,
    His mien was sombre and his mood irate,
Matted and torn his mane, and swollen all
    His mighty limbs.   Anxieties of State !

PART II.

The lordly Lion Haroun one day
    Beneath a shady wood,
A solitary lounger lay
    In meditative mood.
From public cares retired,
    But not from care releast,
Of life, and all things, tired,
    The noble-minded beast
Oft sadly sigh'd, the while he eyed
    The summer grass and flowers ;
And, sighing, heard each happy bird
    That piped from pleasant bowers
To gratulate its brooding mate
    On June's unclouded hours.

Then forth there came, from out of a vine
    That round an elm did range
Her garlands green and globes of wine,
    A little creature strange.

It was of the Monarch's million
Loyal subjects, doubtless, one.
    But never before that minute
Had the Monarch noticed the little creature ;
Uncouth of form, minute of feature,
    And yet, with something in it
That seem'd to strike and harmonise
With the cause of the Monarch's moody sighs ;
    And the Lion's eye-glance tarried
On the pinnacled house, with its painted face,
Which, at a slow and a solemn pace,
    The Snail on his shoulders carried.

Doubtless that tiny householder
    Guess'd not what kingly eye
Did on his movements then confer
    Its royal scrutiny.

For on, with smooth important motion,
He paced, as though he had a notion
    That he was lord of all the way.
His house upon his back he bore,
And on his forehead standards four :
    Erect and proud were they.

To him (thus travelling leisurely,
Unconscious of the Lion's eye)
   Across the path made haste.
Another, smaller, wayfarer,
Swifter-footed, swarthier,
   And slim about the waist.
Then these two mutes, perceiving each
The other, in their native speech
   Did one another hail,
And with familiar salutation
Fell into close confabulation,
   The Emmet and the Snail.

Haroun, the Lion, understood
(As all good sovereigns do, or should)
The dialects and languages
   Of his provincial subjects fully.
And, glad to escape the weary stress
   Of thoughts morose and melancholy
Which did just then his mind oppress,
He hail'd with silent satisfaction
The chance of finding some distraction
In listening to the chatterings
Of such small folk, on such small things
As cabbage-leaves and pips of pine,
And weather-changes, foul or fine ;
In short each ordinary matter
Of such folk's ordinary chatter.

PART III.

The little Emmet shook his head :
  "O Caracol ! O Caracol ! *
I would not be the King," he said,
  " In such bad times." (With prescient soul
Haroun the Lion prick'd an ear.)
  " Why, neighbour, why ? " said Caracol.
" Ah, Caracol ! ah, gossip dear,"
  The little Emmet still ran on,
" You stay-at-home, you'll live and die,
  Not dreaming what great things are done
In the great world. But, gossip, I
  Go gadding here and there, you know,
And many a thing upon the sly
  I pick up that's worth knowing." " How ! "
Quoth Caracol, " good gossip say,
  (I am, indeed, a perfect stranger
To what you hint at,) tell me, pray,
  Is, then, the Empire now in danger ?
From what ? Explain, friend, if you know,
Domestic brawl, or foreign foe ?
  A puissant King have we ! "
" No, Caracol—I'll tell you—no,
From civic brawl, and foreign foe,
  The Empire still is free.
But, ah ! dear gossip, if you knew,
You never said a thing less true—

* The Spanish for snail is here used as a proper name.

The King's *not* puissant."—" He !
What mean you, friend ?" said Caracol.
(Haroun suppress'd a scornful growl.)
   " I mean—upon my life,
   'Tis true," the Emmet said, " the King
Can rule his states—rule everything,
   But his unruly wife.
The King's not master of the Queen,
She masters him. And, this I mean,
   That, master'd by his spouse,
At home he is not puissant—nay,
Not even—the plain truth to say—·
   At home in his own house.
I know a secret gallery
All thro' the palace ('tis thereby
   I pick up odds and ends.)
Ah, if you knew what goings on !
What shocking, shocking things are done,
   What hosts of private friends
The Queen receives upon the sly !
   Poor King ! I'm sure I pity him."
Said Caracol, " And so do I !"
   The Snail's small optic nerve was dim
With sympathetic moisture. " Why,"
Sigh'd Caracol, " what's after all,
Such greatness worth ?" The Emmet small
   Resumed, " Without rebuff
We rule, friend, you and I, our spouses,
Nor fear to enter our own houses.
Abroad, the King, indeed, looks great :

All envy him his power and state.
 At home, he's small enough !

"O Caracol ! my Caracol !
I would not, trust me, for the whole
 Broad realm that he calls his,
Be that unhappy King." " Nor I !"
Said Caracol with glistening eye,
 " My house my castle is.
And, gossip, you and I can say
(What, ah ! *he* cannot) day by day,
 Tho' not in palace dome,
On purple couch, but humble bed,
Each lays his undishonour'd head,
 ' Master am I at home !'"

PART IV.

Roaring with wrath and outraged pride,
 Haroun, the lordly Lion, sprung.
The little Emmet slipp'd aside,
 And hid himself the grass among.
 The Snail, who could not go so quick,
Pull'd his four timorous standards down,
 Swallow'd himself, and (terror-sick)
  Was to a mere saliva grown.

The royal Lion, in its base distress,
 The wretched creature saw,

He could have crusht it into nothingness,
    With one stroke of his paw.
In a cold sweat lay Caracol.   No doubt,
    Master at home was he.
But master *of* his home, he now found out,
    'Twas harder far to be.

Howbeit, happily for Caracol,
    Haroun the Lion, with a lion's whim,
Or else a monarch's scornful self-control,
    Pass'd onward, musing, and so harm'd not him.
" A worm," the Lion mused, " an abject clot
    Of animated slime, that creeps infirm,
Is lord in his own house...and I am not ?
    Well...be it so !   The worm is still a worm.
I am a king.   Bah !...burrow and crawl...become
    One with this earth's obscurest denizens,
To be...as they are...each in his own home
    Master...of what ? mere subterranean dens,
Or flimsy tenements...where they abide,
    This—a sick jelly without even a spine,
That—a grimed drudge?"   And the great Lion sigh'd
    Sadly..." O Leontine ! O Leontine !"

XLVII.

THE PLANE AND THE PENKNIFE.

A LITTLE Penknife, with sore toil and pain,
   In unskill'd hands, was desperately trying
To smooth a great rough plank against the grain.
   "Cease, little fool!" that frustrate labour spying,

A Plane exclaim'd "I'll show thee how to do it!"
   And gallopading up and down, he raced
Nimbly along the plank, as tho' he knew it
   And found the rough work pleasant to his taste.

Like curdling foam, small shavings here and there
   Bubbled; and where the swift Plane flitted o'er
The hard wood, waxing bald, its shaven hair
   In yellow ringlets floated to the floor;

Leaving reveal'd, in delicate design,
   The section'd surface of each wavy vein
And rosin-colour'd ring with fringes fine.
   Then, proudly pausing, "There now!" cried the
     Plane.

"How shall I ever thank thee, friend, enough?"
     The Penknife, much admiring, made reply,
And from his tender blade some notches rough
     He wiped, like teardrops from a grateful eye.

"Thou shalt not thank me, little fool, at all;
     But do thy proper work as I do mine."
The Plane in accents magisterial
     Said to the Penknife.   "Carve thou figures fine

"In lucid maple; or, at most essay
     Thy tender tooth on the ambitious box,
That deems himself as brave, in his own way,
     As elephantine ivory.   On blocks

"Of his unfeatured flesh do thou engrave
     Rare pictures delicate with dainty lines.
To beautify some poet's gentle page,
     Or solace Science with mysterious signs:

"Or round about some richly-foliaged frame
     Wreath, rope, and cherub, sculpture, gay with gold,
To enshrine the image of a high-born dame
     Limn'd by the painter's peerless art of old.

"For this thou *canst* do, and this cannot I.
     And in our family the rule holds good
That each must do his best to justify
     Steel's born superiority to wood.

" The Axe, our father, in the forest wages
 Stout battle with the centenary oaks ;
And they, the giants of a hundred ages,
 Sink groaning underneath his sturdy strokes.

" Ho ! ho ! the crash, when the old warrior goes
 In at them, and their rattling harness, plied
By his reiterated ponderous blows,
 Bursts into faggots ! That is iron's pride.

" The Saw, our mother, when she's set agoing
 Goes thro' it bravely, with a right good will.
Once let her show her teeth, and there's no knowing
 What dust she'll make about her in the mill.

" The lazy trees that lounged about the wood
 And scarce bestirr'd themselves the whole day long,
She turns to trusty planks for service good.
 I, the strong firstborn of our parents strong,

" Less strong than they are, am yet strong enough
 To finish the good work by them begun.
Too tender *thou* art for such labour tough.
 Thou, brother, thou, the old couple's youngest son,

" Since strength thou hast for nothing else, be thou
 At least an artist. We are of the few
Born each, to make a mark i' th' world, and show
 There's metal in us. To thy birth be true."

MORAL.

Plain-spoken the Plane is,
   And somewhat o'erweening
But noble his strain is,
   Since noble its meaning.

Noble utility
   Only is able
To boast the nobility
   Praised in this fable.

XLVIII.

THE DRAG AND THE WHEEL.

1.

Click ! clack ! with a whoop and a whack !
The way is white, and the woods are black.
Thro' glare and gloom, now in now out,
What are the dust and noise about?
In the cloud o' the dust, in the clear o' the day,
What is it comes from the hills this way,
Creaking, recking, heavy and hot,
Downward, townward, What is it?   What?

2.

The road is steep from the mountain-tops :
Zigzag, lower and lower, it drops,
Slanting, sidling, fantastically
Down to the inn by the brook in the valley ;
Whence it runs straight as a road can run,
Half in the shadow and half in the sun.

3.

Rumbling, grumbling, lumbering slow,
With a hi-gee-up! and a hi-gee-wo!
In the white o' the dust, in the heat o' the day,
'Tis a loaded wagon that comes this way.
And its heavily-harness'd horses four
Pant and smoke as they stop at the door
Of the roadside inn, to rest them awhile;
For the team, since morn, hath been many a mile.

4.

While the grooms were giving the horses drink,
The wagoner loosen'd the ponderous link,
Lifted the glowing Drag, and again
Hung him up by his iron chain
Behind the wagon, 'twixt wheel and wheel.

5.

That Drag was shodden with stoutest steel;
But his rusty shoe was half worn away
By the flinty ruts which had day by day
Been rubbing him bare, as, clutching it still,
He carried his wagon-load safe down hill.

6.

So now, as he swung there high and dry,
"Ouf!" groan'd he, "what a drudge am I!

'Tis a pretty sort of a life I lead !
Bearing the burden and staying the speed
Of a wagon with ten good loads at least,
Of timber atop ! each stupid beast
Tugging away the more for me,
And the stupid wheel, with its bandy knee
Dug into my ribs, still doing its best
To be turning round when it ought to rest !
And what reward have I had of it yet ?
Do good to others, small thanks you get !
For, look at these useless Wheels here (nay,
Useless, said I ? far worse are they !)
If they had their will they would soon upset
Wagon, and timber, and all !   And yet
Tho' the wagon is saved by my wise prevention,
It is only they that receive attention.
Do their spokes fall out ? they are reinstated.
Do their axles creak ? they are lubricated,
Greased, and eased, and coax'd to be quiet.
Do their tires fall off ? they get new ones by it,
And go braced with a bran-new iron band,
Brave as (bright arm'd by his lady's hand)
Some knight sallies forth to the tournament,
Whiles I, each bone of whose back is bent
In their service, wearing myself away,
Get never a thank-you night or day
For the care without which (woe is me !)
Soon would the wagon in pieces be."

7.

One of the Wheels to the Drag replied :
" Moderate, prithee, thy boastful pride,
Thou who dost moderate other folk's speed,
Doing naught else in the world, indeed !
Times (I acknowledge it) now and then
Happen to us, as they happen to men,
When our virtues are, for a while, defects.
But 'tis so with the world's best intellects ;
And those times are rare.   I have heard men say
There be water-wagons, whose perilous way
Is over the sea.   When it blows great gales,
Their wagoners then take in the sails,
And throw out the anchor ; putting the drag on,
And stopping the wheels of the water-wagon.
But say, are the sails no use at sea ?
Is the anchor the sole thing needed ?   We
Are as good by land as, by sea, the sails :
And, as good as the anchor is for the gales,
Is the Drag for the hill-sides—going down.
But the gales and the hills are exceptions, own !
To each his merit ; but none need brag.
More often the Wheel is of use than the Drag,
As you'll see in a minute."

8.

The beasts were fed :
The wagoner jump'd on the wagon, and said,

" All right !" and away with no fear of a fall,
Started the wagon, and horses and all,
At a brisk merry trot o'er the long low road
That wound thro' the valley, so smooth and broad.
The dust flew up, and the sparks flew out,
The wagoner smack'd his whip with a shout,
" Hu ! hu !" and the wheels went round :
'Twas a pleasure to see them get over the ground.

9.

Their motion, mockingly, made the Drag
Like a pendulum this way and that way wag.
He seem'd, with a shrug of contempt, to say, " Prithee
Go along, silly world, and the devil go with thee !
Hustle me ! justle me ! flout me still !
My turn will come—at the turn of the hill."

10.

He was right. His turn came round at last :
And pass'd away—when the hill was past.

XLIX.

A HAUGHTY SPIRIT BEFORE A FALL.

PART I.

1.

" BLIND, blind is fate ! unjust and hard my lot,
　　Who bear the burden of oblivious days
Unnoticed and uncheer'd from spot to spot
　　By dull and difficult ways !
How enviably doth the blissful bird
　　Bathe her free life in sunshine and sweet air,
Earth's lightest elements, and undeterr'd
　　Roam the wide welkin !   There
Sublime she wanders with delighted mind
　　Thro' heaven's high glories—I but guess, debarr'd
From contemplation of them.   Fate is blind,
　　Unjust my lot, and hard ! "

2.

Thus, tired by slow and weary pilgrimage
　　Along a short, smooth, easy road, complain'd

A Tortoise ; resting ere the last long stage
    To his near goal was gain'd.
Head, feet, and tail i' the dust, he lay spread out
    Self-crucified, a star that no light gave.
Deep-buried in himself, he bore about
    His own life's living grave.
Yet dream'd he ever of a great existence,
    Where, in lone lorddom over sea and land,
Sun-crown'd and girdled with the azure distance
    The monarch mountains stand.

3.

Then suddenly the ambitious dreamer found
    His sordid life uplifted.   Like his mind
Sublime his body soar'd.   His native ground
    Sank as he rose i' the wind.
And underneath the wide world opens round him.
    The silvery windings of the waters shine
Like little sinuous snakes.   No limits bound him
    Save the broad heavens divine.
The sprawling woods that seem'd immeasurable
    Clump themselves into definite dark shapes.
The light green meadows lengthen.   Skyward swell
    Grey curves of mountain capes.
Deep in cold hollows of extinguisht fire
    Sleep the intense blue tarns.   Sharp points of snow
Glitter, and valleys green with ice-fields, higher
    Than other green things grow.

The pure caress of airs, tho' keen not harsh,
    Cool in the calm of that etherial height
Fan the delighted dweller of the marsh,
    Thrill'd by unwonted flight.
A second Ganymede some second Jove,
    Seeking for beauty here on earth misknown,
In him hath haply found, and borne above
    To the Olympian Throne.
So deem'd the dupe of his own blind ambition,
    And cried, " O my prophetic soul, at last
The Gods repent !   Accepting Fate's contrition,
    I do forgive the past."

PART II.

1.

And tho', indeed, no Ganymede
    The beast was, yet 'tis true
That Jove's own bird on him conferr'd
    This god-like point of view.
For, as of old, some bandit bold,
    Baulk'd of his promised prey
(The Bishop's self with bags of pelf)
    Might grumbling bear away
The Bishop's Fool whose limping mule
    Belated lags behind,
So, missing aim at nobler game,
    An Eagle chanced to find

The torpid beast ; unfit to feast
  His Eaglet brood, but still
A trifling toy which they, for joy
  And not for food, might kill.

2.

As in the Eagle's claw
  The Tortoise upward sail'd,
His flight a Swallow saw,
  And, " O beware !" she wail'd,
" Against thy nature's law
  Why hast thou rashly rail'd ?
Poor denizen of dust,
  Confide not in the fate
Which doth exalt, and must
  Destroy, thee soon or late.
Be warn'd in time : mistrust
  The contact of the great."
" Error !" that dupe replied.
  " The patron who in me
My latent genius spied
  Respects it, tho' it be
By unjust gods denied
  What they bestow'd on thee.
Thanks to his recognition,
  I lack no longer now
The long-desired condition
  Which gives to such as thou

Their freedom, and position
  Above the world. I know
That on the restoration
  To me, and to my race,
Of that exalted station
  Which we were born to grace,
Depends the whole creation.
  Till then all's out of place."

PART III.

1.

And, tho' his listener long ago was gone,
And to the empty air he spoke alone,
Still he continued, with important tone.

2.

" Scorn not the form by dædal ages made
  For my adornment and the world's devotion,
In symbol of the fixt foundation laid
  For the world's motion !
The first word of creation was Testudo,
  And all was in the word. My sire grandæval
Bore on his back (as easily as you do
  Chafer or weevil
In beak or claw) the elephant gigantic,
  Who bore the whole world's weight upon his own.

Wild Change, the revolutionary antic,
  Was then unknown ;
Then, based on principle, the world stood fast ;
  And when the changing world to changeless me
Repentant turns, then all shall rest at last
  Where all should be.
You others are as wanton as the weather,
  Respecting naught. But truth survives neglect.
I wait, and hug myself, and keep together
  My self-respect.
Who knows ? The old Saturnian times return :
  Order I bring, and peace, to earth again,
When tipsy Fortune from her tilted urn
  Shakes down " . . . .
                 Just then
His evil star, on which he had not reckon'd,
Wink'd, and a Hare into the open beckon'd.
    The Eagle spied the tempting prey,
    Unclasp'd his claws, and, well-a-day !
        As swift as crash
        Succeeds to flash,
    When thunder-clouds together clash,
    A swooning fall, a sounding smash !
    And on the earth, it was his vain
    Tho' brave ambition to sustain,
        Shatter'd the Tortoise lay.

PART IV.

The friend that warn'd him in his hour of pride
　　His downfall spied.
The modest bird, with fondly flutter'd breast,
　　Flew to the nest
Which she, who throws in sport o'er sea and land
　　(Beneath it spann'd)
The aëry bridge so exquisitely light
　　Of her bold flight,
Builds, safely shelter'd under low-thatch'd eaves,
　　Of clay and leaves.
There did she mourn, " Mistaken aspiration
　　Is self-damnation.
He who himself hath misappreciated,
　　Is twice ill-fated.
For what his nature never may attain
　　He pines in vain,
Whilst in his natural home, whate'er it be,
　　A stranger he !
Ah, hadst thou known the world as well as I,
　　Ne'er from on high
Wouldst thou have fallen, but hadst lived content
　　As nature meant.
Thee doth desire impel to thine unrest,
　　Me to my nest."

I.

THE ROSE AND THE BRAMBLE.

THERE was a garden—no matter where—
The world is full of such gardens.   There
Flowers of all colour and odour grew ;
And, whatever their odour, whatever their hue,
The gardener gave to them each alike
What for each was good.   In congenial ground
He set each seedling to shoot and strike ;
Each sprout he cherish'd and water'd round
With the self-same vigilance everywhere,
Tended each bud with the self-same care ;
And, nevertheless, in colour and scent,
They came up, all of them, different.
Each had something that best became it :
Each had some quality fair and fit :
Each had a beauty whereby to name it :
Each had a merit to praise in it.
One by its leaf, and one by its stem,
This by its colour, and that by its smell,
These by their blossomy diadem,
And those by their fruit, did the rest excel.

But when that garden was open'd, those
Who walk'd there, turn'd, as they wander'd by,
With one accord to admire the Rose ;
And the rest of the flowers could guess not why.
For " Each flower's a flower," they all averr'd,
" And the Rose is *only* a flower we know."

Now the praise bestow'd on the Rose most stirr'd
The surprise of a Bramble that happen'd to grow
Quite close to the Rose. And he said, " We have
          grown,
Since we were seeds in the same soil sown,
Ever together, the Rose and I ;
And I never could find out yet, I own,
What there is in her to catch men's eye.
However next Spring, it shall be my duty
To find the Rose's secret out."

The Bramble felt not the Rose's beauty,
And he thought, " 'Tis her manner of growing, no
          doubt.
One has but to notice and do the same."

So the Bramble, as soon as the next Spring came,
Noticed ; and saw that the Rose's stem
Was all cover'd with thorns ; and " Oh ho !" quoth
          he,
" 'Tis the thorns that do it ! But we'll beat *them*,
And the world shall see what the world shall see."

·Then, by checking the natural circulation
Of his proper sap in a few May morns
The Bramble, ambitious of admiration,
To imitate Roses put forth thorns.
Yet still, as before, to admire the Rose
The folk pass'd by him. "Good folks," cried he,
"These thorns of mine are more sharp than those
That roughen the rosebush. Turn, and see !"
But nobody heard what the Bramble cried,
Or a passing glance of approval cast him.
Then, to catch the notice, the Bramble tried,
By catching the skirts, of all who pass'd him.

Which attempt succeeded too well, indeed.
For the folk then noticed the Bramble, crying,
"Gardener, away with this troublesome weed,
Which tears our clothes !" And the gardener, spying
The cause of complaint, "Not in all my life
Was I ever disgraced before," he said,
"By such a sad eyesore !" whipping his knife
Out of his pocket; and soon, half dead,
With his feelers all by the roots uptorn,
On the other side of the garden wall
Was the luckless Bramble flung forlorn,
To fare as he might there, thorns and all.

The Bramble ruefully shook his head,
And "What in the world does it mean ?" he said.
"May I be blighted if I can see
What the difference is 'twixt the Rose and me !

One thing alone have I understood :
That what in a Bramble is taken ill
In a Rose is reckon'd all fair and good.
But the reason why is a mystery,
And of vying with Roses I've had my fill."

Then the Bramble crawl'd away to the wood :
And there in the wood you may find him still.

LI.

DUCUNT VOLENTEM FATA: NOLENTEM TRAHUNT.

1.

A MAN, who lack'd even means to make amends
By health and hope for lack of wealth and friends,
Having no tie to life save pain's harsh tether,
Resolved to end both pain and life together ;
And leapt into a river to fulfil
That woeful purpose, when, against his will,
Another man, rich, happy, hopeful, young,
Whilst listening to the bridal bells that rung
Blithe recognition of his marriage morn,
Fell into the same river. Both were borne
Adown the stream ; whose wave, indifferent
To different causes, rolling onward went
To reach the same effect ; regardless which
It drown'd the first, the poor man or the rich.

2.

A Sage, who happen'd to be passing by,
And saw those two men drowning, was thereby
Thrown into a long train of thoughts, profound
And rapid as that river.   At one bound,
The recollection that he could not swim
Came in the first thought that occurr'd to him.
The second from the first as swiftly flow'd
As wave from wave, and, by reflection, show'd,
Concerning those two miserable men,
Who to their deaths were drifting close in ken,
That, if he tried to help them, there might be,
Instead of only two drown'd bodies, three.
His third thought was, that 'twas no use at all
To run in search of aid, or even call,
Since, long ere aid could reach them, even if found,
The wretches must infallibly be drown'd.
His fourth thought, which at once he acted on,
As being the sole thing proper to be done
Without delay, was to elucidate
To these two victims of the force of fate
Fate's ways, by force of prudent precept.   Now,
Tho' how to swim he knew not, he knew how
To talk in Latin.   That was his profession.
And, (being himself in safe and sound possession
Of all his wits) as loud as he was able,
He, in the words which introduce this Fable,
" *Ducunt volentem fata*," with a shout,
" *Nolentem trahunt*," from the bank bawl'd out.

3.

And was it chance, or was it intuition ?
Vast were the treasures of his erudition ;
But from the stores of truths which he possess'd
(The one half serving to refute the rest)
That Sage, by dint of long and deep reflection,
Could not have made a luckier selection,
For, whilst Philosophy thus took her stand
Calm, as became her, upon good firm land,
The truth which she proclaim'd, (put out no whit
By plentiful cold water pour'd on it)
Her influence proved ; awakening there and then
In the damp'd spirits of those drowning men,
This thought : that, if Fate treats the self-same way
The willing and unwilling, whether they
Resist or yield, the end's the same end still,
And bootless both, to will or not to will.
Its next result inverted that conviction,
Proving the force of truth by contradiction,
Philosophy's chief triumph !   Thus, the first
Of those two men, who, with a will athirst
For sudden watery annihilation,
Had jump'd into the river,—tho' natation
Was not to him an art unknown, forewent it,
Letting his body, as the current sent it,
Drift will-less down the water, and from *volens*
Became, comparatively speaking, *nolens.*
The other, who was in the same position
Against his will, exerting strong volition,

Tax'd all his wits to compensate to him
The sad chance of not knowing how to swim;
Call'd to his mind the bride who now no doubt
Was wondering what her bridegroom was about,
Imaged her loss in his; and, fortified
By fond emotions, strove against the tide
With such a vigorous valour that at length
He reach'd, and caught, and clutch'd with all his
    strength,
The lean arm of a weeping willow tree;
Which o'er the water stoop'd, and seem'd to be
Already making solemn preparation
For his appropriate funeral oration.
Tho' much it wept, the willow's nerves were strong:
The man, meanwhile, cried lustily and long.
And, since 'twas not in Latin that he cried,
But that plain language everywhere employ'd
By living creatures to express joy, pain,
Or need, a ploughman on the neighbouring plain
Heard him; and, understanding from the sound
That some one was unwilling to be drown'd,
Ran to the rescue.

4.

        Much at the same time
The first man floated to a bank of slime
Insensible, and stuck there: by and by
Came to himself again: sprawl'd up: shook dry

His dripping rags : and, as the latest word
Which, ere his senses left him, he had heard
Was said in Latin, shivering as he dried him,
The wretch sigh'd ruefully " *Non bis in idem !*"
Then clamber'd to the shore with trailing tread,
Slunk home, and sank, unsupper'd, into bed.—
There, long in miserable plight he lay,
Rack'd by an aguish fever night and day.
But, since he could not pay the doctor's fees,
Gratis the man recover'd by degrees.
And now, one miracle another follow'd ;
For by the last disease the first was swallow'd,
Just as one nail drives out another one.
Feeling his health and strength restored, anon,
Ere he set out in search of work, the man
To brush and clean his sand-caked clothes began.
When, lo you, yet another miracle !
The best of all.   For, glittering as they fell,
The grains of sand that off his garments roll'd
Were mixt with grains of veritable gold.
The poor man sought the well-remember'd bank
Which for his cold, and gold, he had to thank.
'Twas all auriferous.   He tested it,
But kept the secret—and the gold, till bit
By bit a little capital he got.
Therewith the bank he bought, and on the spot
Built workshops, hiring out of many a land
Workmen to wash the wealth from that rare sand.
Plenteous the profit was, since pure the gold.
And thus the man, at last, grew rich—and old.

5.

One day, came, footsore, from a distant Shire
A workman asking work.   Well worth his hire
The stranger proved.   A sober man was he,
Hard-working, honest.   Tho' he seem'd to be
By something nobly mournful in his mien
For better fortunes born, yet staid, serene,
And silent, he his daily taskwork plied.
With curious gaze full oft the master eyed
This stranger: whom one day, when work was done,
He sought, and, at the setting of the sun,
Found by the river bank, with tearful eye
Watching a willow tree that wept thereby.
"Thou sufferest, honest friend?" the good man cried.
"I, too, have suffer'd.   Trust me."   Faintly sigh'd
The other (answering not) "O willow tree
Ducunt volentem fata . . . woe is me . . .
Nolentem trahunt!"   Much surprised to hear
Those words, once heard before with drowning ear,
The master ask'd, and learn'd, at last, what we
Already know.   With this much more: that she
For whose sake this poor wretch had saved his life
That life had fill'd with misery, shame, and strife,
And at the last had left him, leaving not,
To reconcile him to his ruin'd lot,
Fortune or friends.   Thus had he lived to hate
That luckless hour when he, at strife with fate,
Had won the victory.   "Friend, forget the past!"
The master cried.   "In mine a home thou hast.

Nor wife have I, nor children.   Be mine heir.
Who art mine only kinsman, I declare.
For kinsfolk of a sort we needs must be,
Two fishes out of the same water, we!"
Then, when the other hesitated, "Nay,"
He added, laughing, "Fate will have her way.
So, *nolens volens*, it must needs be so.
Shake hands upon it.   There's no saying no,
When Fate saith ay."

6.

              Conversing thus, the two
Whom Fate so strangely had united now
By land, as once by water, by and by
Bethought them of the Sage who from on high,
When each was floundering in the flood below,
Had graciously vouchsafed to let them know
A truth; which he, for the occasion, took
From Seneca; who stole it from the book
Of some Greek Poet; who had borrow'd it
From some one else; to whom some other Wit
Had lent it first.   So, forth the two friends set
To find the Sage to whom they owed this debt.
Him, after fruitless search for many a day,
They found, when he was being borne away
To his last resting-place.

              Where, as 'tis fit,
This story also ends.   No fable it;

Albeit not on that account a fact ;
Since every fable must have to it tackt
Some sort of moral.   But such tales as these
May serve for morals, if their readers please,
To all those fabulous things which so confound us
By really happening in the world around us.

LII.

SUUM QUIQUE.

1.

IT was the hour when woods are cold
   And there is no colour in all the sky,
Because night's blue is gone, and the gold
   O' the dawn not coming till by and by :
It was the hour when vapours white
   Are over the dark meer rolling slow
From the brewage brew'd by the water-sprite
   Who inhabits the sunless deeps below.

2.

In the reed and rush, 'twixt meer and fen,
Two wild white Swans were fighting then ;
For a wild white Swan-Bride fighting keen ;
The lake's two lords for the lake's one queen.
And altho' both woo'd her, but one could wed,
   And but one be victor, tho' both fought well.

And the vanquisht warrior, wounded, fled
　　Foom the wrath of his rival peer, and fell,
　　Over the reed-fenced rivage damp,
　　Into the filth of the fenny swamp ;
Whence the sound of his funeral hymn rose clear
From the marsh to the woodland, and over the meer.

3.

Thro' the reeds he crushes, from the forest rushes
　　The bristly bulk of the fierce Wild Boar ;
Crashing down bud and bush, pashing the mud and
　　slush,
　　And scattering filth from his cleft feet four.
And " Who is it that calleth for help ? " quoth he.
　　" Here, all who enter my subjects be.
Let the wronger beware ! and, if fight he can,
　　Fight for his life, or fly with speed !
Eh, . . . but, bless my bristles ! . . . a Swan ?
　　And, if I mistake not, a Swan indeed !
Welcome, Cousin !   Allow me, pray,
To ask what weather blew *you* this way ?
　　Or is it, O lord of the lucid lake,
(Thou stateliest swimmer !) that thy white neck
　　Is weary of watching each snowy flake
Of its whiteness imaged without a speck
　　　In the over-perfect purity
And tedious calm of the crystal flood ?
　　And hast *thou*, too, learn'd, at last, to sigh
For the common, but more congenial, mud ?
　　Hah ! by each buffalo's cloven crest

In the herd of them put to flight by me,
    I swear (for I love thee, noble guest!)
I will share mine acorn crops with thee,
    If thou, contented, a swine with swine,
Wilt change those too-white plumes of thine
            For the bristles and hair
                We hogs do wear.
    Already, thy haughty beauty wanes!
        Fallen, tho' unresign'd, art thou.
    And the spurted slime of the fen's drench stains
        That princely bosom of spotless snow.
Thou that immaculate swammest the meer,
Wallow in mud, and be welcome, here!"

4.

    Bleeding, aching, weary, and wan,
    Bitterly listen'd the noble swan,
To those brutal words; and "O shame and grief!
    He moan'd, "that in such a place—to me—
And with such a speech—the ignoble chief
        Of an obscene herd should dare to proffer
            His fulsome friendship filthy and free,
    And a swan be shamed by a swinish offer!"

5.

        With failing breath,
        On the threshold of death,
            By an effort vast
        (His saddest and last)

He arose ; and, quickly
    Staunching his wound
With the grasses sickly
    That grow on such ground,
Sprang forward ; crying
    " St Pelican !
I die ; but, in dying,
    Am still a swan !
St Pelican hear me,
    And grant my cry !
In death be near me,
    And let me die
As I lived, at least,
A swan, not a beast,
In mine own pure element's purity ! "

6.

The Saint reprieved him.
The wave received him,
And, washing the stain from each wounded limb,
On his deathbed bathed and rebàptised him.

7.

Then, backward turning his stately head,
On the haunts of those he had scorn'd and fled
    He gazed ; and saw with a dying eye
      Afar in the forest the filthy herd,
Profaning its sacred groves, rush by ;
    And the mirth of the wallowing monsters heard.

And " Each to his own !" the Wild Swan said,
  " And his own to each ! and I to mine !
As the Swan to his purity, so to his bed
  In the mud he was born for, returneth the Swine.
For, if a Swan fall in the filth of the fen
  Where the dew turns slime and the green grows
    sallow,
And even the strong foot slips, what then ?
  He doth but fall where the Swine doth wallow.
        Suum cuique,
          To live or die :
        Hic et ubique
          A Swan am I ! "

LIII.

THE TWO TRAVELLERS;

OR,

LOVE AND DEATH.

WE are not made for Beauty, nor for Love,
　　　Nor for Eternity,
Perchance.　But something in us, from above,
　　　Yearns to embrace all three.

Lost in a silent land of winter wild,
Where, warming nothing, yet on all things smiled
　The eternal snows that lit that lonesome land,
　Two weary travellers wander'd, staff in hand,
Over the frozen hills.　Fast friends, together
They two had fared thro' fortune's changing weather;
And each had loved; and each life's common chance
Had curst with war 'twixt love and circumstance.
But in that conflict, one to love, that claim'd,
　Had yielded, all : whilst one life's fate had freed

From love's embrace ; and, struggling forward, maim'd
  In every feeling, saved, not all, indeed,
But all mere life hath left when love is dead,
  And dead, with love, life's sense of lovely things.
Now, as they wander'd weary, round them spread
  (To make more weary still their wanderings)
  Endless tranquillity. And all the while
  Above them, and about them, everywhere
  Along the land and in the leafless air,
  Throughout that region of unblest repose
  They felt the fixt unsympathising smile
      Of the eternal snows.

    It was the smile of Eternity,
  That smileth, whether men live or die.
    Every sorrow, and every joy,
    Every pleasure, and every pain,
  Hath something—it may be, all—to dread.
But, with nothing to lose, and nothing to gain,
  Eternity smileth the smile of the dead.

  " I have seen the Sphynx in the Desert " said
    To his fellow-pilgrim one of the twain,
  " And the smile upon Nature's face, methinks,
  Is as the smile on the face of the Sphynx :
  The smile of indifference ! Death smiles so,
  And so smiles Love—on the loss and woe
  That waste the hearts of his human prey
When, having o'erwhelm'd them, he passeth away

As they sink in dust, to smile down for ever
From his unattainable heaven so high
On the generations, whose foil'd endeavour
Cannot interpret, however it try,
Nor answer, save by a feverish sigh,
That inscrutable smile, with its unsad Never!
For Love is Love, for aye, as of old :
And, Spring by Spring, as the leaves unfold,
Lives shall blossom in Love's strong sun
That beameth for all, and abideth for none.
But Life is mortal, tho' Love be not,
And Death is, was, and shall be.
And Nature heeds not her children's lot,
A wanton mother is she!
Friend, I am tired, and can no further fare.
Here will I rest."—"Ah, madman!" cried the other,
"Here is but Ruin with Rest's face. Beware!
Shake off this fatal lethargy, my brother!
'Tis Death that woos, and not Repose,
The weary and unwise
To his cold couch in these deep snows.
Poor wretch, arouse! arise!
Some succour, sure, must be at hand,
Some issue from this dreadful land.
For lo! where leans yon woodland high
Along the windless air,
Some woodman's hut methinks I spy,
Or charcoal-burner's rude repair,
A smoke is in the frosty sky.
Deliverance must be near!"

" Ah, brother, prithee let me be."
His comrade answer'd.   " Whither flee ?
Deliverance ! . . . dost thou seek it ?   See,
    'Tis at our feet—'tis here !"

And, as he spake, he sank.   With a shrill cry
The other turn'd, and fled : from peak to peak
Springing, and clinging, dizzily, foot and hand.
The upland forest, heavy, huge, and high,
Seem'd slipping o'er him from its icy shelves.
And, wildly mocking the man's human shriek,
    With most inhuman revelry,
Outleapt the echoes of that lonesome land,
    Like mad malignant elves.

O'er the giddy steeps he climbs, he leaps,
    And his breath is salt with blood.
And there's blood in the skies—or blood in his eyes—
As, with reeling steps, and choking cries,
And broken strength, he reaches, at length,
    The Woodman's hut in the wood.
And his voice doth seem like a voice in a dream
When he shouts and beats at the Woodman's door,
    Faint and blind as a wasted wind
    That beats its life out, trying to find
    Its lost way over a moor.

    " Ope, Woodman ! ope
    For charity !

Help ! help ! a rope,
  A hand !   Hard by
On the nether slope
  Doth my comrade lie,
Lost, if no hope
  Of help be nigh,
For I can no more.
    Wake, Woodman ! wake,
And open the door
  For Jesu's sake ! "

" Come hither ! come hither ! " the Woodman cried
To his four sons, " and bear him inside,
  And pile him a bearskin bed,
And cut the boots from his swollen feet.
  These famisht pulses feebly beat,
    But the poor wretch is not dead."
So the Foresters chafed him, limb by limb,
  Till, feebly, again, in each frozen vein
  The life-blood ran ; and the rescued man
    Felt Death's fingers releasing him.
His lips they bathed in the cordial cup,
And, alive at last, they lifted him up ;
But leaving in Death's grip, lost and gone
Life's ransom—claim'd by the hungry cold,
Which had bitten his flesh to the very bone,
So that what remain'd of the man thus saved
  Was a ruin—horrible to behold,
On whose living flesh Death's mark was graved.

Then this living half of the half-saved man
    The search after his lost friend began,
Whom he, and the Foresters, found at last
    Sunk in the drifted snow, beneath
That desolate upland vague and vast,
        Dead—but beautiful in death.
And over the dead man's face was cast
The smile of the Sphynx : that smile which is
      The smile of indifference.   Seeing this,
        He that saw it recall'd the past.

When, long since, they twain were young,
    And, as together they journey'd along
Life's unknown, and yet untried, way
    Love o'ertook them, and seized his prey,
The dead man there, now calm, and fair,
With a mighty effort had broken Love's snare,
    Giving to him, the survivor now,
      The self-same counsel, to struggle on,
He, himself, had refused, when he sank in the snow,
    And gave up the ghost ere the goal was won.
    Not so of yore ! when, with tears, he tore
His tortured spirit from Love's control,
    But thus left for ever behind him, lost,
The finest and fairest parts of his soul,
    Saving the rest of himself at their cost.

Now, he lay dead, with the smile on his face.
    Dead, but unblemisht, and fair in death,

And, over his features calm, the grace
    Of a peace unbroken by mortal breath.
Maim'd in feature, and crippled in limb,
The living man look'd down upon him;
And, fair, in the dead man's face (with awe
Because of its careless beauty) he saw
The image serene of his own dead soul.
Dead—but in death still beautiful!

LIV.

AN ILL-ASSORTED COUPLE.

1.

THERE was a couple who could not agree,
  Tho' conjoin'd by a fate they were forced to obey.
And of one of that couple the name was HE,
  And the name of the other did HE call THEY.

2.

Different in age, as in all, were the two ;
  The youngest HE, and yet ages old ;
THEY even older, and short of view,
  As of hearing hard, if the truth be told.

3.

HE was resolved (and some sages say
  It is man's best study) to study himself ;
Taking small heed of his yokemate. THEY
  Spared no abuse of the self-will'd elf.

4.

"He," said They, "is the bitterest brute!
    A bear,—and his bearish actions show it."
Which opinion settled beyond dispute,
    'Twas a miracle only could overthrow it.

5.

But falling sick, and recovering slowly,
    He grew as tame as a brute could be;
And, his rebel habits reforming wholly,
    Meek and mild as a lamb was He;

6.

Doing whatever a lamb can do
    To evince the virtues for which man love it:
Whilst They, disinclined to opinions new,
    Cried "He is a bear, and his actions prove it!"

7.

Hard of hearing, and short of sight,
    Thus They took . . . was it ten years, or more?
To discover that all was at last lamb white
    In the blackness so bearishly black before.

8.

Truth, however, will find her way
    To the dullest brain, if you grant her time;

And so after thus chiming its ten years, THEY
  Changed of a sudden this chiding chime.

9.

" HE," at last said THEY, with no doubt at all,
  " Is the sweetest soul.   We have wrong'd him, we.
And that was but honey we took for gall."
  Meanwhile (what was it sour'd him?) HE,

10.

Because HE had tried and had fail'd to please,
  Or because of original sin, once more,
A backslider, became by unblest degrees,
  The unsocial bear he had been before.

11.

Yet " HE," cry THEY, and still go on crying,
  " Is the sweetest soul, and his actions show it!"
Do THEY believe it, or are THEY lying?
  One thing only is sure.   I know it.

12.

Between a man and his reputation
  There is a space to be travell'd thro':
And when rumour reaches its destination
  The tale it tells is no longer true.

13.

Each ray of the star you are praising to-night
    Hath been long on its way to your world below :
And your praises, perchance, are bestow'd on the light
    Of a star that hath perish'd an age ago.

LV.

BETWEEN HAMMER AND ANVIL.

(A SONG OF THE IRON AGE.)

1.

THE bellows, breathing, fann'd the forge :
Forth sprang the thrill'd white sparks in throngs :
The Young Smith from the furnace gorge
Pluck'd out between his pinching tongs,
And flat on the resonant anvil laid,
The red iron, ablush with a radiant glow :
The Old Smith, dealing it blow on blow,
With his ponderous hammer the hot mass bray'd.

2.

And, whilst about it son and sire
In mutual mirth their business plied,
The iron, weeping tears of fire,
To hammer and to anvil cried

"It is iron ye be, yet, O torturing two,
It is iron ye torture!"   But "Suffer thy lot,"—
They replied to him, "fool, and upbraid us not;
For there's some one above us is dealing the blow."

3.

Oh had the Old Smith, whirling fast
His hammer, heard that talk?   For, gay
He, thro' the roar o' the furnace blast,
Laugh'd "*Divide et impera!*"
"*Amen! Amen!*" the iron replied, giving vent
To a groan, as it grew to a sword.   This, anon,
To its place in the arsenal pass'd: and the son
Of the Old Smith into the army went.

4.

One day the town's bad blood broke out.
The artizans arose in arms:
The Civic Guard they put to rout,
And fill'd the streets with fierce alarms.
But the soldiers came cantering into the town:
And, with patriot pride in so loyal a job,
Slashing this way and that as he rode thro' the mob,
A young soldier by chance the ringleader cut down.

5.

"My son!" the giant gasp'd; and heard,
As grovelling in his gore he lay,

A captain, who had given the word,
Laugh " *Divide et impera !* "
" *Ámen ! Ámen !* " the Old Smith responded ; and died
As the Young Smith, unnoticing, flourish'd his sword.
Revolution was ended and order restored
By the youth's unintentional parricide.

6.

The King then went to war.   Long while
His stricken subjects rued that day.
The foeman gain'd by gold and guile
One half the misruled realm away.
Thus, against itself upon all sides turn'd,
Did the gash'd land bleed at each gaping pore :
They but meant it well, the two armies swore :
Meanwhile they ravish'd, and robb'd, and burn'd.

7.

And in the last great fight of all
The Old Smith's soldier son expired.
His ribs were broken by a ball
From his old Captain's pistol fired.
But, before the last breath of his life he breathed,
He resolved, at the least, not to breathe it in vain ;
And the sword that erewhile had his father slain
In the breast of his leader lost he sheathed.

8.

The conquering General rode that way,
Glowing and fierce as Mars' own Flamen,
Laugh'd " *Divide et impera !*"
And gallop'd onward. "*Ámen! Ámen!*"
With a finger sly on his Golden Fleece,
(While the General gave his moustache a twist)
Responded the smiling Diplomatist
Commission'd to settle and sign the Peace.

9.

The Peace was sign'd : and, having wrought
The conquest thus confirm'd, elate,
The Military Party thought
Itself the master of the State.
But the Diplomat, hiding his own intent,
The Generals, jealous and fierce, inflamed
With a rival hope ; and the fools proclaim'd
A Republic ; that chose him as President.

10.

For, whilst with faction faction fought,
The moderate man slipp'd in between ;
The votes of either party bought,
And baulk'd them both. More calm and keen
Than the rival chiefs that around him vied,
When the popular choice he had charm'd away

The rogue laugh'd " *Divide, impera !* "
Praising himself with a secret pride.

11.

Yet, tho' so soft the whisper'd word
He, laughing in his sleeve, let fall,
Its secret boast one listener heard ;
Who, unobserved, observing all,
Behind him stood with a downcast eye,
And a serious smile on a meek lip set,
As " *Ámen !* " he mutter'd, and softlier yet
" *Ámen !* " again, to his rosary.

12.

The Young priest, he, to whom by choice
The dame, whose charms in private bless'd
That charmer of the public voice,
The weakness of the flesh confess'd.
Thus craftsmen and soldiers and clerics and laymen
Do the burden pass, as they pass their way :
And the burden is *Divide impera !*
And the response to it is *Ámen ! Ámen !*

13.

Sic semper ! Iron still is dasht
On iron : blood on blood. The hours
That rock the round world, rolling clasht
From the high tops of temple towers,

Are the hammers of Fate : and they fall and fall
Heavy and fast on the anvil of Time ;
Where Humanity changes its shape as they chime,
And, save only in shape, never changes at all.

14.

'Twixt hammer, thus, and anvil bruised,
  The wretch upbraids that torturing two ;
And they reply, the oft accused,
  " There's one above us, deals the blow."
Who is it, then ?   History's intricate page
Can but reckon the strokes, and record the gravamen.
Stat pro ratione voluntas.   *Ámen.*
This is the song of the Iron Age.

LVI.

HOMO HOMINI LUPUS.

1.

Some villagers who in their trap had caught
  An old sheep-stealing wicked Wolf at last,
Resolved that he to trial should be brought,
  And judgment in due form upon him past.
And since no Counsel could avail him aught,
  Because in fact his sentence was forecast,
  The Court, considering his case a grave one,
Most graciously ordain'd that he should have one.

2.

They might have hang'd or headed him at once
  Without this legal circumbendibus,
Since he was in their power for the nonce.
  But Justice loves, as cats do with a mouse,
Not to make all at once her final pounce
  Without some fond preliminary fuss
Of indecision.   So the Court decided
A Counsel for the Wolf should be provided.

3.

A man as full of learning as a book,
   A scientific traveller much respected
By all the worthies of that rural nook
   Where he awhile was lodging, they elected
To this good office: which he undertook
   Well pleased, since he for the accused detected
Much to be urged.   No harm the Wolf had done
To flocks or herds of his.   The man had none.

4.

The Prosecutor's speech, as it behoved,
   Was most laconically eloquent.
" For, since the Wolf's a wolf, my case is proved."
   Said he, avoiding needless argument.
Thro' no superfluous details he roved,
   But to the point with plain precision went,
And cut his speech short, keeping to one head,
The Wolf's ; which must be cut off too, he said.

5.

Upon the utterance of this demand
   The Culprit's learnèd Counsel show'd his teeth ;
The Wolf's teeth, not his own, you understand.
   And goodly teeth they were ; above, beneath,
Two rows of daggers formidably plann'd
   Their shining blades in flesh and blood to sheathe.

" And you'll admit," he said, " one fact is plain :
Such tools were never made for grinding grain.

6.

" But, as your shears for shearing wool were made,
 Which is the purpose that you put them to,
So were the teeth set in this creature's head
 For tearing flesh ; and he employs them so.
What is there in such conduct to upbraid ?
 The Wolf is innocent. He does but do
As Nature bids him ; whom obey he must.
Then cut off Nature's head, if you'd be just.

7.

" This beast, moreover, ('tis no merit small)
 Is one of the best parents in creation.
I, therefore, for the Wolf's acquittal call,
 With damages to boot, and compensation
From you his judges and accusers all,
 For false imprisonment and defamation."
The Judges and the Jurymen were, each
And all, at first struck speechless by this speech.

8.

But soon, with sense of scandalised propriety,
 They left the Wolf, his Counsel to assail ;
For language quite subversive of society,
 And doctrines which, if suffer'd to prevail,

Would place all honest folks in great anxiety,
    Despite of gallows, constable, and jail.
Science escaped, sore bruised, from this affray,
And the sly Wolf, ill guarded, slipp'd away.

9.

The Culprit and his Counsel being fled,
    No case remain'd before the Court. " I ween
Never was such ill luck ! " a Juror said.
    " That rogue, the Wolf, would certainly have been
Condemn'd on every count, to lose his head,
    But for this most discreditable scene.
For, what in our assemblies is so rare,
This time we were unanimous, I'll swear."

10.

" Friend," said another, " then you'll swear too much.
    Peter would still have voted against Paul :
First, since by nature, or by habit, such
    His practice is ; and next, since, after all,
He knew his counter-vote could work no touch
    Of difference in the sentence, great or small.
Some men there be who vote in opposition
Always, with safety, upon this condition.

11.

" The mischief is that, having now been told
    By that subversive scientific knave

That he is in his natural rights, made bold
   Thereby, the Wolf is likely to behave
With even greater licence than of old ;
   And, fill'd with self-conceit, will fiercely crave
The free indulgence of a natural right,
To satisfy his wolfish appetite."

12.

" Nay, neighbours," said a third, " you are, indeed,
   Too hard upon the Doctor. By the way,
Who was it, Martin, cured thy cough unfee'd ?
   Who mended Peter's pump ? And who, Paul, say,
Taught thee, by crossing, to improve that breed
   Whose fleeces fetch'd the highest price to-day ?
Ye took his counsel then, which now you spurn
Because, forsooth, it serves another's turn.

13.

" He said the Wolf was right to be a thief,
   And that is going far too far, say I.
But then, he added that the Wolf's the chief
   Of all good fathers of a family ;
Which gives the lupine character relief.
   That touch'd me, and should touch us all. For
     why ?
These dangerous characters have still a heart ;
By which to win them is the statesman's art."

14.

So spake the Village Schoolmaster.   He had
   A numerous family himself.   In all
Nine children, counting in the good and bad
   Together, and the big ones with the small.
A fellow-father-feeling made him sad
   That even a rascal's family should fall
Into starvation ; and his eyes grew dim,
For his own eloquence drew tears from him.

15.

As for the Wolf, so far as can be guess'd,
   Nothing by all this praise and all this blame
In him was alter'd.   It must be confess'd
   A common error to think words make tame
Or fierce such creatures.   Wholly unimpress'd
   By all our talking, they remain the same.
A wolf's a wolf: and nothing you can say
Will change him, tooth or teat, say what you may.

16.

Good talkers, flatter not the hungry crowd.
   All your soft words will butter it no bread.
Yet speak the truth, nor spare to speak it loud
   For fear lest Hunger's clamour to be fed,
Acknowledged just, should wax too fierce and proud.
   Words change not facts.   Friends, cut off Hunger's
      head :
There'll be no wolves to fear, or flatter, then.
If not ; beware of hungry wolves—and men !

LVII.

THE HORSE AND THE FLY.

1.

A HORSE-FLY stung a Coach-horse in the nose.
　The Horse, with pain and terror of the bite,
Rear'd, and (despite the Driver's cries and blows)
　Upset the coach ; and gallop'd out of sight.

2.

Side by side together, knitting
Happy hand in hand, were sitting
In the coach, when it roll'd over,
Maiden-bride and Bridegroom-lover.
　　By a pair
　　More fond and fair
Bridal vows were never spoken :
　　And already rose in view
The sweet home they were journeying to,
When the Bridegroom's neck was broken,
　　And the Bride's heart broken too.

3.

The Coachman, from the coach-box thrown,
Dash't out his brains on a boulder stone.
The honest fellow behind him left
A widow and orphans five bereft.

4.

Fast and faster the Horse, poor brute,
Flying in vain from the feign'd pursuit
Of the goading pang his own flesh hath in it,
And fiercely quickening at each wild minute
The impetuous speed of his desperate paces;
Whilst clamorous after him clatter the traces
Which trail'd thro' a whirlwind of dust, he drags;
(With flat ears back laid, and red nostril flay'd,
And flanks foam-oozing, that heave and smoke)
Gallops into the town, gallops over the flags,
Where, to left and to right in precipitous flight,
He scatters the startled and terrified folk.

5.

After drifted blossoms straying,
Birds and butterflies waylaying,
Down the street a Child is playing:

Springing, singing, for pure joy,

All the world his pleasant toy;
A fair, rosy, bright-hair'd boy.

6.

And the people shout, and the people cry:
And he hears the noise: but he knows not why
The others are shouting, and he shouts too,
For the joy of mere noise, as a child will do:
And the galloping horse gallops over him.
And that pretty Child (but a minute before,
Life's merriest minim, all mirth and whim)
Now a palpitant ruin bedabbled in gore,
With bright head bleeding and broken limb,
The people bear to his father's door.

7.

That father's only child was he:
Lost heir to a princely pedigree:
Last fruit of an old ancestral tree.

8.

Alas, what sufferings from a single cause!
How many wrongs, how many miseries!
What misdeeds punishable by no laws!
Who was the guilty author of all these?
The Horse? But what responsibility
Have horses for their conduct, even when

No horse-flies bite them? Not the Horse? The Fly?
    Well, but the Fly's misdeed? what was it, then?

9.

Maternal love that Fly obey'd.
Her eggs in Nature's lap she laid,
And, moved by mother-instinct, tried
For her own offspring to provide.

10.

Maternal Love, then, must we call
Sole author of these mischiefs all?
If so (at least on moral ground
Which some folks hold the only sound)
Methinks 'tis easier (search and try them)
To make laws than to justify them.

LVIII.

ET CÆTERA ET CÆTERA.

1.

I saw a man die, miserably. Death
    With lips disdainful of such sorry fare
(Like one who, sauntering thro' his orchard saith
    ' The fruit, tho' flyblown, that lies rotting there
Must needs suffice me ') nibbled the remains
Of life ; which long disease, with parching breath
    Had ravaged so, that Death was doubtful where
To bite what look'd no longer worth his pains.
Naught of the wretch was left but sores and brains.

2.

And nothing in this corpse-about-to-be
    Seem'd living yet but life's last beacons, two
Bright feverish eyes, whence life defiantly
    So fierce was flashing, that Death, fain to know
What meant their dumb defiance, render'd back

A moment's breath to set the man's lips free;
    As hunters on a dying fire do blow
For light to guide them on their dubious track,
Ere they fare onward thro' the midnight black.

3.

Then, to Death's question, the death-rattle cried
    " Long perishing I lived.   On pain I fed.
I had no children, and I had no bride,
    Like other men.   But with Disease I wed,
And this, mine own death-hour, on her begot.
Yet all so well, against life's woes allied,
    My solitary soul, from heel to head,
Was arm'd in patience, they subdued her not.
What she hath wrought can neither rest nor rot.

4.

" For in me a sublime idea hath lived;
    In me, and on me.   What was I?   Its food,
And dwelling-house.   I perish : but it thrived,
    And shall thrive.   I have given it flesh and blood.
That flesh and blood is mine.   My whole life long
Was for the good of this idea contrived,
    And all mine ills have but increased its good.
Non omnis moriar !   I still prolong
My power in this, whose life mine own made strong.

5.

" For there it lives—in yonder leaves—complete !
   Where yesterday these feverish fingers wrote
The last word : not what crowns the closing sheet
   Of vulgar volumes with appropriate note :
Not FINIS, my life's labour's last word was.
Because I doubt not of my guerdon meet,
   Because the life, whereto did I devote
Mine own life, here no mortal ending has,
Therefore my last word is ÆTERNITAS.

6.

" Yes ! mine idea shall live, bright, beauteous, glad.
   In me all's weak, but where is weakness here ?
In me all's sorrow, here is nothing sad.
   Clouded my life was, but my thought is clear.
The Spirit that thro' formless space did flit,
Seeking fit form, its budding purpose clad
   In a child's brain, and breath'd in that child's ear
' Child, my thought chooseth for its servant fit,
Live for it, labour, suffer, die for it ! '

7.

"That child was I, and I obey'd. Alas,
   I lived to die. But, dying, I set free
A life that's deathless. Into dust I pass
   Content, because the thought that lived in me

Lives and shall live. 'Tis well. My work is done.
Finis for me : for it ÆTERNITAS ! "
    That was the man's last word. His work and he
Are both forgotten. Underneath the sun
Naught is eternal save Oblivion.

8.

I saw a chrysalis. It hung beneath
    My lattice eaves. I watch'd with hopeful eye
The bright release of that embodied breath,
    The dead worm's destined beauteous butterfly.
I tapp'd it, and there came a hollow sound.
In Sleep's similitude, already Death
    Dreaming the birth of a new life did lie.
I broke its shining shell. And there I found
Another chrysalis within it bound,

9.

But swollen big, and just about to burst ;
    A second and surprising chrysalis,
Whose growth had eaten hollow all the first,
    Which it would soon have shatter'd. What was
        this?
The egg of an ichneumon : who, within
The moth-grub's miserable frame, had nurst
    Her bastard babe, and fed on borrow'd bliss
Its being, buried in her victim's skin
Pierced, for that purpose, with a cloven pin.

10.

The first eruca, thus, the second fed.
  Sic vos non vobis ! The poor moth-grub pined.
The young ichneumon in the moth-grub led
  A prosperous life. Upon the patron dined
The client, well. The moth-grub labour'd sore,
And starved. The ichneumon lack'd not board or bed.
  The second flourish'd as the first declined.
The moth-grub died. The ichneumon lived the more,
Wanton and wing'd, and livelier than before.

11.

Doubtless that moth-grub knew not its own state :
  Felt deep disquiet, and divined not why :
Was proud, perchance, that in it something great
  Grew, and grew greater. Was it haunted by
Ambitious dreams? Meanwhile with toil intense
It must have labour'd, to emancipate
  The life within it. Thus, its enemy,
And idol also in a certain sense,
The poor fool fatten'd at its own expense.

12.

And did it, when it wove its death-shroud, say
  (Poor worm, that ne'er a butterfly might be,
Whose past was pincht, whose future filch'd away
  By that which lived within it !) even as he

Whom I saw dying, did it say, " I pass,
My work remains. The Spirit I obey,
   As fittest out of thousands, fixt on me
For that sublime idea whose slave I was.
Fixis for me : for it *ÆTERNITAS* ! "

13.

Ah, ' fittest out of thousands ?' Yet behold !
   The ichneumon which upon this worm did prey
Will find just such another worm to fold
   The egg it is its wont in worms to lay.
And from that egg will soar another fly,
Which, in its turn, will do as did the old.
   And thus *et cœtera, et cœtera,*
Et cœtera, which, far as we can spy,
Is also Latin for Eternity.

14.

Patience hath of ichneumons pointed out
   As many as three hundred different kinds,
All living on as many kinds, no doubt,
   Of different insects : as, on different minds,
Different ideas. Brains, we must avow,
The strongest, cannot yet *per annum* sprout
   Three hundred new ideas ; and man finds
The old ones troublesome. But troubles grow,
And even the weakest brains breed notions now.

15.

Meanwhile, whenever I behold a man
   With burthen'd forehead, bald before his time,
And visage, like a lamp at noontide, wan,
   Who thinks, by nourishing some thought sublime,
To pay himself, in death, life's many pains ;
And, having spent his strength in prose or rhyme
   On some idea which hath been the ban
Of all his being, boasts " My work remains,"
I muse " What maggot hath he in his brains ? "

LIX.

MONUMENTUM ÆRE PERENNIUS.

1.

Two neighbours from each other claim'd a field,
And neither of the two his claim would yield.
Wild words between them pass'd. These nothing
    skill'd.
Blows follow'd words ; and one of them was kill'd.
The dead man's kinsfolk then together came,
Sworn to do justice : and did just the same.
That is to say, they did a second time
What, done the first time, they had judged a crime,
And slew the slayer. From these deaths arose
'Twixt tribe and tribe long strife of living foes ;
Who in the dead men's quarrel fought, until
Which of the dead men did the other kill
Was by their hostile progeny forgot ;
And neither side could quite remember what
Each side was fighting for, tho' generations
Prolong'd the conflict, and at last two nations

In arms opposed each other.   The sole aim
And end of all such conflicts is the same,
Whether two peasants or two peoples fight :
Each from the other strives to wrest the right ;
Each on the other strives to wreak the wrong ;
And each, as both the varying strife prolong,
Is vanquisht or is victor, turn about.
For, as " the whirligig of time " whirls out
Alternate chances, is the vanquisht race
Avenged on the victorious.   In this case,
Born of the conquer'd tribe, arose (men say)
After long centuries had roll'd away,
A conqueror : who, in half a hundred fights,
The wrongs of his slain fathers to the rights
Of their more fortunate sons converted; slew,
And led to slaughter, thousands; but o'erthrew
The overthrower, and to dust beat down
A secular oppression.   Tower and town
Tumbled in smoky ashes, heaps of bones
Pasht and in a bloody puddle, gasps and groans
Of masht-up men, a mass of different deaths
Mixt with a murmur of admiring breaths,
Founded the FIRST eternal monument
Which in men's memories made this last event
Imperishable ; and, with gush of gore
And glory from men's minds for evermore
Wiped out the first, poor, perishable, mean
Cause of the conflict, which thereby had been
Crown'd with immortal claim upon the praise
And retrospective pride of after days.

2.

To many a lyre by many a lyrist strung,
About the land that hero's deeds were sung.
And many a homely lay, from door to door,
From sire to son, repeated o'er and o'er,
Transmitted to a far posterity
Traditions of his worth.   But, rolling by,
Time, in its unretentive current, brought
New interests, new desires, to thrust from thought
The rusted image of the Heroic Age;
Whereof this monument remain'd to wage
War with Oblivion.   Vainly; till, by chance,
Its mouldering record caught the fervid glance
Of one who, haunted by a name forgot,
Raked in old legends long remember'd not
For glimpses of that name; which, like a star
Flashing mysterious splendour from afar,
Brighten'd the abysmal past.   Its fading beams
This poet mingled with his own fresh dreams,
And wrought therefrom, to renovate renown,
A poem which the whole world for its own
Claim'd and forthwith immortalised.   Thereof
(As, from the music of Amphion, rough
With topless towers, arose in circuit strong
The Theban ramparts raised by rolling song)
A new eternal monument was made:
Whose glory cast into oblivious shade
(Or in its brighter self absorb'd anon)
The lesser lustres of the former one.

For, from this fresh eternal monument
Gracing the threshold of an age, were sent
Memnonian melodies and echoes far,
Waked by the radiance of the rising star
Of a new art more beautiful than war.

3.

The old eternal monument, meanwhile,
Whereof naught rested but a ruin'd pile
Of names and dates (mere useless rubbish reckon'd)
Had furnish'd forth foundations for the SECOND.

4.

And all men deem'd the Poet's work to be
More lasting than the Hero's.   Nathless, he
Who wrote the poem which, by men proclaim'd
Immortal, made its mortal parent famed,
Had died of want in some obscure small town.
Men search'd, in vain, the empire up and down
To find his birthplace ; and, not finding it,
(Tho' many volumes were to help them writ,
Each volume proving hopelessly absurd
Whatever by the others was averr'd)
The baffled seekers by degrees began
To shape the ideal image of the man
Out of his song ; imagining a face
And figure suited to his spirit's grace.
The State, then, order'd that this image, cast
In ever-during bronze, should be at last

Erected in the imperial capital
On a tall pillar; to be seen of all
Who there, throughout the ages, came and went.

5.

This was the THIRD eternal monument;
Which all the previous monuments effaced.
And the great poet's name, upon it traced,
Was read by multitudes who read no more
The old-fashion'd verses whence that name of yore
Its immortality of fame received;
Which from Oblivion nothing new retrieved
Save the bronze image, on whose marble base
His name still figured, in the market place.

6.

Long while this third eternal monument
Struggled with time, and the wild weathers bent
On its destruction. But it felt their strength;
And, bit by bit, the rain and rust at length
Wore out the graven words and sculptured frieze.
The image, also, dwindled by degrees.
One day the lightning struck it, and it fell.
At least, so saith the civic chronicle
Which is our warrant (since we cannot show
Proof more conclusive) for believing now
That such a statue once commemorated
The birth (by modern critics much debated)

Of such a poet.   Nowadays you see
A brave soap-boiling manufactory
Upon the spot where once that statue stood,
Which made immortal, for the multitude
That moved beneath it in the days gone by,
The poet's unremember'd memory ;
Who sung the imperishable song ; that wrought
Renew'd eternity in human thought
For that immortal hero's deathless name ;
Whose perisht immortality of fame
Rose from the reek of bloody towns ablaze,
Even as the smoke that rises nowadays
From you tall chimney; which yet marks the spot
Where stood the statue men remember not.

7.

These facts we have thought fitting to consign
In the foregoing record, line by line,
To the attention of posterity ;
In order that we haply might thereby
Save all these otherwise entirely lost
Eternities ; which mutually cost
Each other's ultimate annihilation.
Nothing remains of them, but this narration.

8.

And, if this last must be forgotten too
(Leaving no vestige to the future) who
Will owe its author (the FOURTH time, alas !)
' A monument more durable than brass ?'

LX.

SANS SOUCI.

PROLOGUE.

Work! But when can I work, pray, when?
  At morn? I have not yet done my doze.
At noon? But too heavy the heat is then.
  At eve? But eve is the time for repose.
At night? But at night I'm asleep again.
  Work? What is it? As I suppose,
'Tis the vain invention of idle men;
Whom the Devil could help to no happier plan
  For getting thro' time, than this idiot trick
Of adding fatigue to fatigue; like a man
  Who carries his boots at the end of a stick
Slung behind him, to add to the heat
And the weight on his back; as, with limping feet,
  Thro' the flints that tear, and the thorns that
    prick,
He fares barefooted, and boasts he can
  With such bootless trouble get on so quick.

If you chanced, as you wander'd, to meet with a brook
    Flowing among the mountains, say
Would you hasten back to the house, and look
    For a bucket to fetch the water away
Into the valley? Down from the hills
Let the water flow as the water wills.
    When it gets to the valley at last, some day,
        There will it stay, unashamed? or say
        " To work! to work!" and begin with pain
        To run up the hills and back again?
        Enough is doing around it. Why
Should itself be doing aught? The sun
        Reveals to it all that, up in the sky,
The weather is going to do, or hath done.
        The moon will bathe in it by and by;
And the stars, that follow her one by one,
            Seek and discover it,
              Peeping thro'
           Clouds that flow over it,
              Changed in hue
           By winds that o'erhover it,
              Hid in the blue.
           Barks, too, along it
              From shore to shore
           Will wander, and throng it
              With sail and oar.
           Each bending double,
              With sweat o' the brow
           From toil and trouble,
              The rowers row,

But, how fast soever their oars may fall
The water, which takes no trouble at all,
Will still be the first to leap to shore.
And, what is more, when the voyage is o'er,
Will still be as fresh as it was before.

Lie on the bank, then! idly lie
Beside me, watching the wave flow by.
And, if Fancy follow it, heed not why.
Heed not why, and heed not where.
Fancy will find in the summer air
Whatever she seeks, for her home is there.
Let us open our hearts to the summer sky.
From mine I have let this fable fly.
Who knows where it may 'light?   Not I.

PART I.

There were two brothers.   And each of the two
Said to the father of both " Let us go
Forth and away, O Father, from thee.
For the world is fair : and eager are we
To be living there, with a life set free."
And the Father said to his sons " Do so."
But, first (for a mighty magician was he)
" My sons," he said, " the world is wide ;
What in it attracts you most, decide.
And then ask (ye shall get it) the gift of me
Which best for the choice of you each may be.'

And "O Lord our Father," the sons replied,
"Even so! and to each, as the choice, be the dower."
Then he carried them up where, in all its pride,
From the summit serene of a specular tower
Might be descried upon every side
The whole round world.   And, opening at once
The magazines of his manifold power,
He said to them " Chuse, and use, my sons."

The First made choice of a pair of legs.
Stout flesh and blood, no wooden pegs ;
But legs of muscle and sinew strong,
That could do whatever a man's legs can.
" And with these," quoth he, "will I get along,"
As he put them on and became a MAN.
The Second laid hold on a sturdy root,
Pleased with its power of fixing fast ;
Hid himself with it ; and, shoot by shoot,
Became, tho' slowly, a TREE at last.

The man in possession of that stout pair
Of human legs, by the help of these
Trod many a road, scaled many a stair,
Climb'd the mountains, traversed the seas,
Braved strange weathers, and breathed strange air,
Learn'd new manners, new languages,
Saw crowded cities, and deserts bare,
Felt the dogstar burn, and the polestar freeze,
Ransack'd earth for the far, the fair,
And yet nowhere on earth could the man find ease.

For, wherever he thought to have settled, there
Something he noticed which fail'd to please,
Or something he miss'd which had pleased elsewhere.
And the worse he fared the further he went,
For comparison everywhere ruin'd content.
Those legs ran away with him : day by day
Wearing his life out ; and wearing away
His boots ; which to mend, he was forced to spend,
And, in order to spend, was forced to get, .
And, in order to get, to earn by the sweat
Of his brow, the gold which in getting and spending
The man wax'd old ; still wearily wending
That way thro' the world whereunto is no ending.

PART II.

Long tired of that long way, he sank at last
    Worn out upon the wayside sod, beneath
A mighty tree ; whose branches o'er him cast
    Shade that was shelter, haunted by the breath
Of hidden flowers.   A rivulet flow'd past
    From out-of-sight to out-of-sight ; and, flowing,
Call'd out calm sadness from the silence vast
    Wherein hot noon was glowing.
Then did that old man feel thro' all his frame
    A creeping rest.   His legs, whose strength was spent,
Left him at last in peace ; and he became
    Careless and conscious of a vague content.

But, while he follow'd with incurious gazes
  The streamlet flowing where aught pleased it best,
That melancholy, which in man's soul raises
    Emotion born of rest,
Drew from the old man's eyes another stream
(Whose source was in his spirit) of sad tears.
And, as some spot which only in a dream
  A man remembers, who forgets the years
That made it long forgotten, so to him
  Return'd a memory of that mystic minute
When life's choice lay before him, with a dim
    Desire of action in it.

" Alas !" he wept, " what wasted tears
Are these which weep my wasteful years !
And all this while, what have I done
But still from disappointment run
To disappointment? With what pain
What mountains have I climb'd in vain !
What flesh and blood these feet have left
On flinty peak, in thorny cleft !
How many a time these knees and shins
Have suffer'd for their owner's sins !
How often, falling bruised and sore,
With rage have I arisen once more,
To stumble on, I know not where
And know not how—such vagrants were
These worn-out legs ! What have I gain'd,
Who, leaving all, have naught attain'd,
And naught have kept? I wonder how
It fares with my lost brother now."

PART III.

Then sound that, flowing, follow'd sound
  Rippled the leaves above him.
And the branches, bending down to the ground,
  A canopied cradle wove him.

As still as a tired child that is taking
  Sweet rest on its mother's knee,
The grey old man, neither sleeping nor waking,
  Lay under the green old tree.

And was it brother speaking to brother?
  For he heard the tender tone
Of a voice that seem'd not the voice of another,
  Though he knew that it was not his own.

It was sweeter than all other voices are.
  It was not like the voice of a man.
It seem'd so near, and yet seem'd so far,
  And it spake as no other voice can.

PART IV.

Softly it murmur'd " Dost thou know me not,
  My brother?   I, the Forest, I am he,
The one friend left thee in earth's one safe spot,
  Whose love, where'er thou wanderest, waits for
    thee ;

" Outlasting all things for the loss of which
    That love is consolation : gold misspent,
Youth wasted, hope impoverisht, to make rich
    The thankless avarice of discontent.

" Love faithful, love unchangeable, and fast
    As is the root whereby 'tis fixt and fed !
Vainly the world, wherein no root thou hast,
    Thou wanderest seeking what, when found, is fled.

" And think'st thou I am solitary ?   Thou
    It is who art a wandering solitude.
For from thy life away thy life doth flow,
    And, self-pursuing, thou art self-pursued.

" ' Not here,' thou sigh'st, ' I live, for life is there.'
    Yet, hadst thou waited, life had come to thee,
Who, seeking life, hast miss'd it everywhere ;
    Whilst here, where rest is mine, life sends to me

" Momently messengers, that know the way
    To find me, from the world's four corners come.
The winds, and clouds, and stars of heaven, are they,
    And the sweet birds that to my heart fly home.

" Count me the emmets that go up and down
    My creviced bark. Know'st thou what myriads
       move
In any blade of grass o'er which is thrown
    The shadow of my power and of my love ?

" What lurks and crouches under any stone
    That nestles at my feet ?   What builds and breeds
In my least berry ?   Or what deeds are done
    Even by my least distinguishable seeds ?

" The Tree stands steadfast, contemplating all.
    Tree-trunk from tree-trunk earth holds safe and
        single :
But, weaving one etherial coronal,
    Tree-top, in heaven, doth with tree-top mingle.

" What buoyant bridges, which the squirrel knows,
    How airy light, how delicately wrought,
The elm-tree to his beechen brethren throws,
    Where branch with branch is mixt, as thought with
        thought !

" All this the Tree hath of the root he hath.
    For whoso hath no root, no life hath he.
No path leads to him.   And by every path
    He from himself must needs a wanderer be."

PART V.

Whilst thus the mystic voice yet spoke,
Harsher sounds thro' the forest broke.
And men came thro' it, and men came near,
With shoulder'd axe.   " What do ye here

Intruders ?"—" Ho ! we hew down wood.
Idler, make way for Work !"   They stood
Under the tree ; and the axe was laid
To the root thereof; and the tall tree sway'd
To and fro, and then crash'd to the ground.

The old man, stunn'd (but not by the sound)
About him gazed with bewilder'd eye
Over the alter'd earth and sky,
And " What is it," he moan'd, "that is broken in
 me ? "
As he follow'd his brother, the fallen tree.

Follow'd the tree to the timber-yard :
Learn'd the craft of the carpenter :
Plied hammer and saw, and labour'd hard,
Laid plank upon plank, join'd oak to fir,
Till the stately vessel slid from the slips,
Slid from the land, and slid into the sea.
There, with those new-gotten wings of hers,
To wander the waters—a ship among ships,
Who no longer a tree among trees might be,
And (a mariner, there, among mariners)
With the rest of the good ship's crew went he,
The man, not able to leave the tree.

PART VI.

On the sideless seas, in the middle hour
Of the savage and measureless night ; when stars
By curdling clouds were quench'd, and a shower
Of stormy sleet thro' shrouds and spars
Shriek'd ; and the grieved ship seem'd to cower
Under night's weight, as wild she ran
Across the cruel grey waves; the man
Lean'd his ear to the tree (which fast
Stood over him still, a mighty mast)
For the wood, with an inward moan, began
To writhe and heave : till there came at last
A thunderous buffet of wave and wind
That shatter'd the ship.   And, swept by the blast
Into the murtherous midnight, blind
With madden'd weather, clinging together,
O'er the headlong sea the man and the tree
Drifted to shore on a desert isle.

The ship and the crew had perisht meanwhile.
But the man was alive : and the tree (twice dead)
Which had saved him, still protected him.
For of part thereof, to shelter his head,
A roof he wrought ; and each dripping limb
He dried and warm'd at the fire he made
Of the rest of the wood.   And when morning rose
Over the reefs, with ravage spread,

As tho' on a world all newly made,
And smiling, safe from its last birth-throes,
In freshness, sweetness, light, and repose,
The man, left lone in the desert, said
" Oh what a release ! to be left in peace
By all that trouble of tiller and tackle,
The captain's cries, and the shipmen's cackle !
Each rope and sail, and yard and shroud,
That, in calm or gale, no quiet allow'd,
But must ever be shifted that way and this
For fear of shipwreck ; which, all the same,
In spite of our trouble and caution came.
And oh how delicious the freedom is
From all care henceforth of the cargo that's gone,
Or the ship, that is sunk, or the voyage, that's done ! "

PART VII.

Years, long afterwards, mariners, driven
By stress of weather, touch'd on that isle,
Where their ship had found a natural haven
Hidden from howling storms.   And while
The desert, in search of springs, they roved,
In the desert they found a fallen pile
Of spars and planks ; whose structure proved
That a human hand had fashion'd and hewn
That pile, long since by the sea-winds strewn.

And, under the ruins which once were a hut
(Safe from the ruining sea-winds shut)
A dead man lay.   And the dead man's face
Yet wore, in its features worn, that trace
Which a life in the waste cannot all efface
Of a life once lived in busier lands.

The mariners buried with pious hands
That dead man's dust in the desert sands.
And, since they found two spars of a tree
Which none of the island trees could be
(Parts they seem'd of a broken mast,
Haply to shore with the dead man cast)
They set them, crosswise, above the grave
Of their fellow-creature ; in sign of the faith
Which, finding but death in life, men have
That man's spirit is made for a life in death.

It was the last protection that the tree
Could give the man, his brother.
And ah, if helpless that protection be,
What help in any other?

PRINTED BY WILLIAM BLACKWOOD AND SONS, EDINBURGH.

www.ingramcontent.com/pod-product-compliance
Lightning Source LLC
Chambersburg PA
CBHW030322270326
41926CB00010B/1473